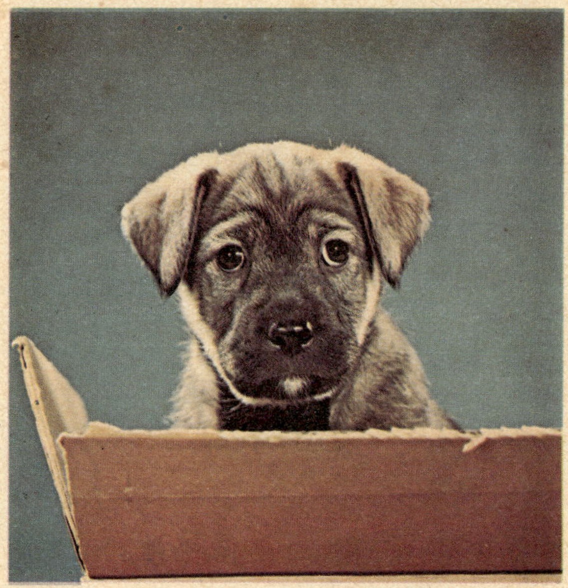

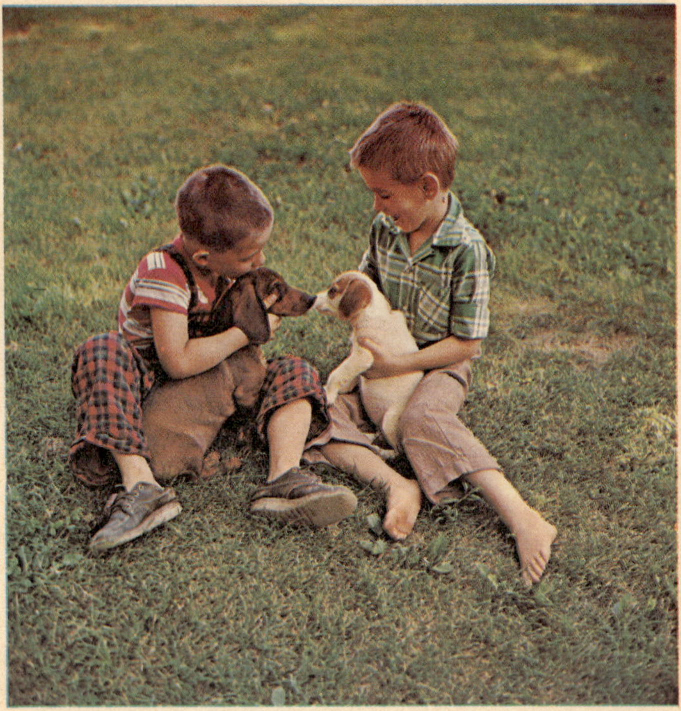

THE Dog YOU CARE FOR

FELICIA AMES

Associate, Friskies Research Center

With 60 photographs in color by
WALTER CHANDOHA

A SIGNET BOOK from
NEW AMERICAN LIBRARY
TIMES MIRROR

Copyright © 1968 by Carnation Company

All rights reserved

SIGNET TRADEMARK REG. U.S. PAT. OFF. AND FOREIGN COUNTRIES
REGISTERED TRADEMARK—MARCA REGISTRADA
HECHO EN CHICAGO, U.S.A.

SIGNET, SIGNET CLASSICS, MENTOR, PLUME AND MERIDIAN BOOKS
are published by The New American Library, Inc.,
1301 Avenue of the Americas, New York, New York 10019

FIRST PRINTING, AUGUST, 1968

8 9 10 11 12 13 14 15 16

PRINTED IN THE UNITED STATES OF AMERICA

CONTENTS

Foreword   *11*

1 : It All Begins With Love

Have You Chosen a Dog You Can Love?	15
The Car Ride Home	16
Welcoming Him (But Not Too Enthusiastically!)	17
Insuring a Good Night's Sleep	19
Will He Be a Doghouse Dog?	20
He Needs Few Possessions — But They Must Be His	22
Now Is the Time to Find a Veterinarian	23
Keeping Your Dog Safe — A Lifetime Responsibility	23
If Your Dog Is Lost	26
His License — Your Protection against Loss	27
AKC Registration	29
Why Not Bone Up On Your Dog?	29

2 : A Polite Dog Is A Popular Dog

Anyone Can Train a Dog	33
Calling Him by Name	34
Number One Lesson — House-training	34
Keeping Your Dog Quiet (And the Neighbors Happy)	37
Leash-training	39
Who Loves a Problem Dog?	47
Some Typical Dog Problems	47

3 : The Dog You Care For Will Be Healthy

Your Dog Should Have Four Shots	57
External Parasites	58
Internal Parasites	59
Skin Disorders	60

6 The Dog You Care For

When Your Dog Is Ill	60
Caring for the Old Dog	64
Your Dog's Medicine Cabinet and First-aid Kit	65
When Your Dog Is Injured	66
First-aid Chart	68

4 : Grooming Is A Part Of Good Health

Your Dog's Grooming Kit	79
Giving Him a Handsome Coat	79
Nails	80
Eyes	81
Ears	81
Teeth	81
Bathing	81

5 : A Well-Fed Dog Is A Healthy Dog

Some Common Food Fallacies	85
Feeding Your Dog a Balanced Diet — The Easy Way	87
The How and When of Feeding	89
Feeding Chart	91
Feeding Your Puppy	92
Puppy Feeding Schedule	94
Feeding the Older Dog	96

6 : To Mate Or Not To Mate

The Female's Season	99
The Male Dog	100
Breeding Your Dog	100
Care of the Pregnant Female	103
Preparations for Delivery	104
The Whelping Day Arrives	105
Now That the Pups Are Here	106

7 : How To Travel With Your Dog (And Not Wish You Had Stayed Home)

| Traveling by Car | 111 |
| Traveling by Air | 115 |

Contents 7

Traveling by Ship	116
Traveling by Train	116
Traveling Abroad	117
Summing It All Up	*119*
Vital Statistics and Health Record	*121*
Index	*126*

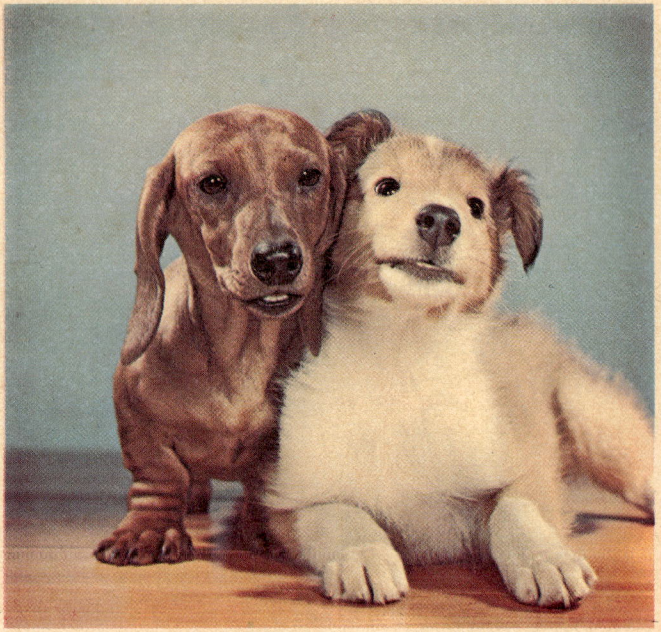

Acknowledgments

This book has been written with the technical assistance of:

Carnation Research Center, Van Nuys, California
  J. M. McIntire, Ph.D., General Manager
  Harry Kimpel, Ph.D., Director, Bio-Med Technical Services
  Lloyd Miller, Ph.D., Manager, Nutrition Research

Carnation Farms, Carnation, Washington
  Erich Studer, D.V.M., Director, Friskies Research Kennels
  Bob Bartos, Manager, Friskies Research Kennels

John D. Chudacoff, D.V.M., Consultant in Veterinary Medicine, Carnation Company

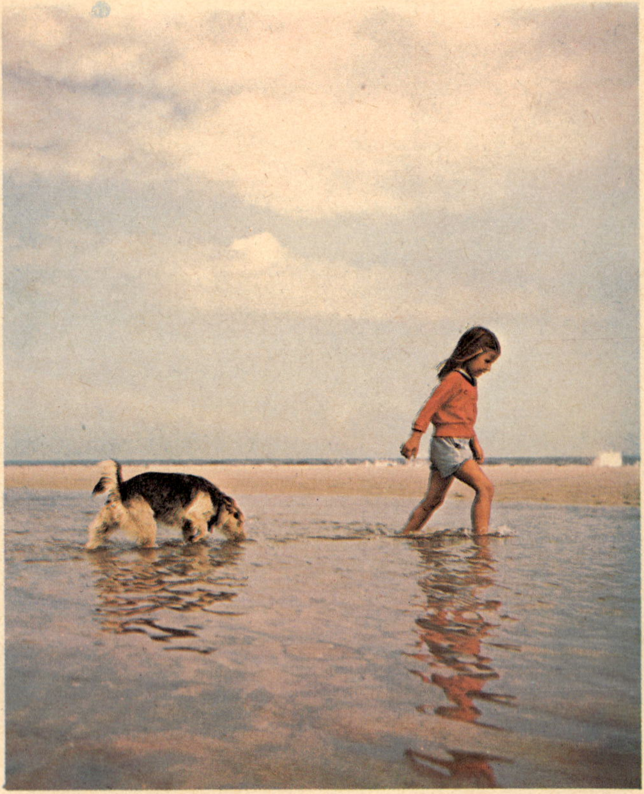

FOREWORD

That's a happy dog you have there! And no wonder. With so many to choose from, you've decided on one very special dog to become part of your family. The lucky pup!

Whether you've chosen a purebred or a mixed breed, your dog will give you pleasure and companionship directly in proportion to the thought, the care, and the love you are willing to give him.

It's your responsibility to love and care for him. You want to *keep* that tail-wagger of yours happy if he is to thrive. The dog, since prehistoric times, has always been the devoted companion of man and dependent on *him*, not on other dogs, for his happiness.

It takes love to make a happy dog — and a lot of knowledge to make that love intelligent. Affection isn't enough. You need *know-how*.

Love for your dog is a big responsibility. This book can help make this new responsibility a joy by giving you the facts you need to feed, train, and care for your new pet in the happiest possible way.

1

It All Begins With Love

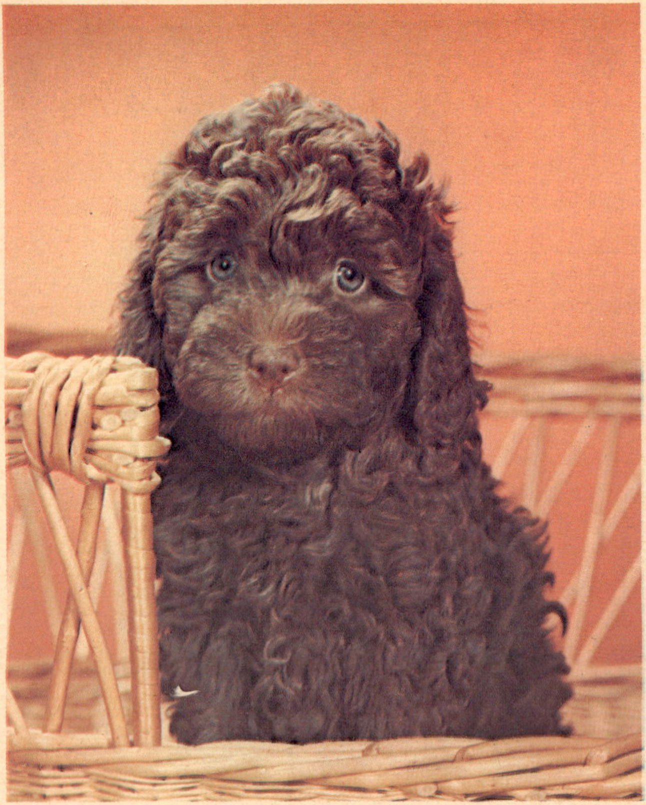

Have You Chosen a Dog You Can Love?

Every dog is lovable to someone. But the dog *you* will love is the dog that fits in with your way of life, the dog whose personality suits yours.

So many factors must be considered in choosing a dog — the size of your living quarters and your yard, the number and ages of children in the family, the way you live, even your own temperament. The apartment dweller usually prefers a small dog; a large family needs an affectionate, patient animal. A man who is easygoing might not appreciate the active attentions of a terrier; and a rugged outdoorsman would probably prefer a hunting dog to a dainty poodle.

Before you take the dog of your choice home, consider the following points to make sure that your new friend won't be making a round trip:

- If you have chosen a large dog, are you sure your yard is big enough and your fence strong enough (large dogs can dig under many fences) and high enough? Will the dog spend much time in the house? Do you have time to give him proper exercise?
- If there are children, does this dog seem relaxed enough to enjoy boisterous play? Is he gentle? Is he old enough to be handled safely by those young, loving hands?
- If you are adopting a female, are you prepared to keep her safe in season so she will not present you with puppies and more puppies?
- If you have chosen an adorable puppy, have you the patience to put up with his not-so-adorable mischief and lack of training?
- Which suits your disposition better — a vivacious animal or a more relaxed one?

- Have you thought about the expense of feeding and grooming this particular dog? (A very large dog may require as much as ten pounds of dog food a day; a tiny poodle costs much less to feed but requires frequent professional grooming.)
- Did this dog greet you in a friendly manner? (It is safer to select a dog that shows enthusiasm for people rather than an indifferent or withdrawn one that may have a somewhat ingrown personality.)
- Does this dog have the clear, sparkling eye, the cool, moist nose, and the vitality that show his health is excellent?

The Car Ride Home

Because you want to get off to a good start with your pet, give careful thought to his car ride home. It is a good idea to have a responsible second person along to hold the dog and reassure him. Taking into consideration all possibilities, you would

It All Begins With Love 17

be wise to put a sheet or towel under the dog to protect your upholstery. You can't blame him for being nervous — maybe you are too!

Check with the kennel or shelter before you leave for any information it may have on your pet, especially in regard to his health record and his shots.

Welcoming Him (But Not Too Enthusiastically!)

There will probably be great excitement when you bring the new dog home, which your dog will sense immediately. If he is a puppy, the unfamiliar quarters and new persons around him may be quite upsetting.

See that the dog does not receive too much attention all at once. Let him quietly nose around and get acquainted with his new environment. Feed him only a light meal.

Although discipline is necessary from the first day, let it be somewhat relaxed until the dog feels secure. (If your dog temporarily forgets he's housebroken, grit your teeth for a day or two until he comes down to earth.) Keep noise and visits from young children at a minimum, and don't let the young ones play too strenuously with their new friend.

If the dog is a puppy, remember — that round furry ball won't bounce, and handle accordingly. To pick him up, place one hand firmly under his chest, the other under his hindquarters. This way you insure that the dog feels, and *is*, secure. Make sure that all children in the family know how to handle the dog before they are allowed to pick him up.

Insuring a Good Night's Sleep

Your dog's first night home may be a lonely one for him, and he may let you know it, especially if he's a pup. You'll rest more easily if you have made some preparations for him.

First make sure his new bed is comfortable. It should be in a room neither too cold nor too warm. Any clean carton or box makes a fine bed for a pup, as long as it is large enough to allow him to stretch. One side should be cut low enough for him to get in and out easily. You may line the box with newspapers if the dog is not housebroken, then put in an old

20 The Dog You Care For

(but clean) blanket, or a small mattress or rug. An older dog does not need to sleep in a box, as long as his bedding is placed in a draft-free spot. *Do make sure that the dog's bed is free from drafts.*

While you should be sympathetic, you must also be firm — so that your dog does not expect you to come running every time he whimpers. A friendly word, perhaps light shining through a crack in the door, will comfort the uneasy dog. A hot-water bottle (not *too* hot) or a glass jar filled with warm water will make a puppy feel cozy and secure. (Do not put an electric heating pad in the bed; a puppy may chew the wires.) Some veterinarians suggest putting a ticking clock in the bed. To a pup this sounds like his mother's heartbeat.

Will He Be a Doghouse Dog?

Now is the time to decide whether your dog will sleep inside or out-of-doors.

If your dog is a toy or a miniature, he should not be housed outside. If you would like your dog to sleep outside but have doubts as to whether or not it would be healthy, ask your veterinarian.

Once you have decided that your dog will be a doghouse dog, the sooner he is acclimated the better. In summer a good-sized dog may start living outside as soon as he is six weeks old. In winter you had better wait until he is seven or eight months old.

His doghouse need not be fancy. Even a crude, do-it-yourself shelter will be a happy home for your dog, provided that it:
- Has a floor raised off the ground, so that no moisture can get in.
- Is twice the length of the grown dog.
- Is protected from wind.
- Has the doorway covered with a baffle or canvas flap.
- Has a removable roof or side for easy cleaning.
- Has some provision for outdoor shade. If you cannot situate your doghouse under a tree, it should have some type of shaded porch where the dog can rest on

warm days. Many dogs like a platform — they can sun on top or burrow into the cool earth beneath.

Once you have put your dog outdoors to sleep, stick to this system. Changes in temperature — from a warm house to brisk air, for instance — can make your dog ill.

He Needs Few Possessions — But They Must Be His

Devote a shopping trip to obtaining all your dog's equipment, modest though it be, so that both of you can enjoy its usefulness right away.

You will need:
- Food pan (one large and shallow enough for the dog to get his muzzle into)
- Water pan
- Stiff brush
- Comb
- Collar (a slip chain for training is fine for all dogs except long-haired varieties like collies)
- Leash or lead (a good link chain is advisable at first, and essential if your dog will grow large)
- A few safe toys (*Note*: Do not give your dog sponge rubber toys; he can swallow the crumbled rubber. Some

plastic toys can also cause trouble. Give him only toys that are too large to swallow and too tough to chew to shreds. Leather toys are best. Nothing painted with lead-based paints should ever be given a dog. The danger of poisoning is too great.)

- His own grooming kit (See page 79 on grooming aids)

Now Is the Time to Find a Veterinarian

Even though your dog appears perfectly healthy, you should take him in for a checkup to be sure all shots have been administered (see page 57 on inoculations) and that grooming needs, such as dewclaw removing and nail trimming, are taken care of. Your veterinarian will also check your dog for worms — which may be present even though there are no symptoms — amd examine his teeth, eyes, ears, and feet.

This first appointment provides a good opportunity to find the veterinarian to whom you can entrust your dog's health over the coming years. Should an emergency arise, it is important to know a veterinarian in whom you have complete confidence, who can be reached after his office is closed.

You can obtain names of veterinarians from your local veterinary medical society or the yellow pages of your telephone directory, but you will probably also want to ask friends for recommendations. You will know on your first meeting if this is the veterinarian for your dog. You can sense by the way he handles and speaks to your dog if he is the one you want to care for your pet.

Keeping Your Dog Safe —
A Lifetime Responsibility

In one sense, a dog never grows up; he remains always a child. For the rest of his life you must think ahead for your dog's safety; this happy innocent will constantly bungle into dangerous situations, both inside and outside of the house. During these first weeks you should check your home and yard for potential hazards.

• If your yard is fenced, make sure there are no holes your dog can wriggle through, that the gate latches firmly, and that those who enter are warned to close it securely.
• If you have no fence, tie your dog in a manner which allows him some freedom to enjoy the yard. A rope attached to a clothesline gives the dog a chance to run and move freely without getting tangled. There are also

It All Begins With Love 25

ringed pegs with long chains for 360° freedom. Keeping your dog confined to the yard is especially important during his first week with you. He's not really sure yet that this is his home.
- Take care to remove ant and snail poisons from the dog's yard. Keep him from plants that have been sprayed with insecticides.
- Check the garage to be sure that paint cans, corrosives, alkalies, and acids are put away on high shelves.
- Clear the dog's yard of small stones and pebbles; some dogs swallow them.
- Keep a sharp eye out for broken glass.

- Make sure that no electrical wires are low enough for your dog to reach. If he bites through the insulation, he could suffer severe, even fatal, shock (see page 74 for signs and treatment of shock).

- Too much sun and heat can harm a dog. Make some provision for shade if the yard has none. Never tie your dog when he is left in the sun.
- Finally, *never unleash your dog when you are walking him on a public street.* The automobile is probably the largest killer of dogs in the United States. Even the well-trained dog will break away from his master and run into the street if the temptation is attractive enough.

Dog-proof the inside of your house, too, before you let your pet wander from room to room — for his safety and your own peace of mind.

- Soaps, detergents, bleaches, and other cleaning supplies should be kept on high shelves.
- Do not leave pills or medicines where the dog can reach them.
- Keep floors clear of needles, pins, and small toys like jacks and marbles.
- Guard your sewing supplies (puppies love needles!). Keep thumbtacks and screws out of his reach.

Most mature dogs will leave these things alone, but puppies will swallow anything they can.

If your dog is a puppy, don't place him on beds or chairs; he may injure himself falling, even from these low heights.

In spite of all precautions you will take, your dog may at some time be injured. Prepare yourself for this mischance now. (See pages 65-75 for first-aid information.)

If Your Dog Is Lost

Even the best-behaved and best-cared-for dogs will occasionally disappear out the gate, unnoticed by the best-intentioned master. What to do then? Get busy fast:

- Ask the neighborhood children.
- If he has been missing several hours, call your local humane society or animal shelter.

It All Begins With Love 27

- Put a sign (preferably with a picture) on the bulletin board of your local school and supermarket.
- If you suspect the dog has been stolen, call the police.
- Advertise in the newspaper.
- Contact your local radio stations. "Pet Patrol," sponsored by The American Humane Association, is solely concerned with finding lost pets.

His License — Your Protection against Loss

Get your dog's license as soon as possible and see that it is securely linked to his collar. Your dog can then be traced, provided you have filled out his licensing paper correctly. You should also attach a metal tag to his collar, giving your own name, address, and telephone number.

Your local humane society or animal shelter can tell you your city's regulations on dog licensing and where to obtain your license or rabies tag. You may also call your city hall for information. All puppies of more than six months of age must be licensed; in some communities this must be done as early as three months.

It All Begins With Love 29

AKC Registration

If you have adopted a purebred dog, you should make the dog's transfer and ownership registration official by recording it with the American Kennel Club, 51 Madison Avenue, New York, N. Y. 10010.

Why Not Bone Up On Your Dog?

There's a lot to know about your new dog! This book provides essential information. In addition, there is excellent literature available at your library and bookstore. It's interesting and helpful to have detailed data about the particular breed you have adopted.

The more you know about your dog the more valuable he will be to you and the more fun you both will have.

2

A Polite Dog Is A Popular Dog

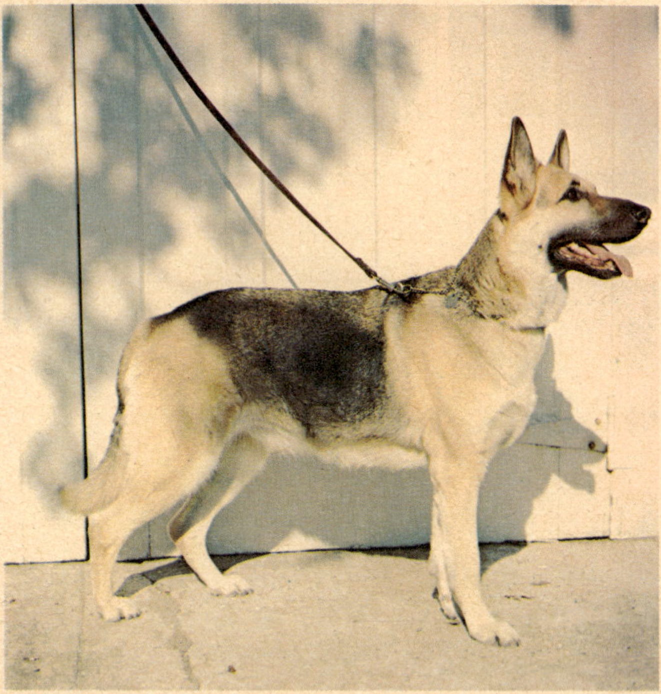

THE biggest favor you can do for your new pet is to begin right away to teach him good manners. Wouldn't you much rather have him liked than merely tolerated (or even shunned) by your neighbors and friends? He must know how to keep his behavior within bounds on all occasions, right down to the smallest sniff.

Strict discipline is not just for show dogs. Nor is rigorous training cruel. All dogs thrive on it. They like to know who's boss. After all, your dog wants to please you and lives for your attention. And when you're training him, you're all *his*.

Anyone Can Train a Dog

Training a dog is all in knowing how. Actually, most dog training is very simple because a dog's mind is uncluttered. Your attitude must be:

- firm
- calm
- patient
- persistent

Effective training can only be brought about by:
- consistent commands
- constant repetition
- warm praise or a tasty treat for commands carried out

Because your training must be consistent, you must first read and memorize each step of training. You cannot be firm in your commands unless you are sure exactly what you want done.

Calling Him by Name

Even a small pup will respond quickly to his name if it is repeated often enough. Give your dog a name of one or two syllables, or one that can be shortened to a syllable or two. The dog probably hears only the first syllable of even a two-syllable name. So if you must call your dog Nicodemus, let him come to "Nick."

When you are training your dog, you will often couple his name with your commands: "No, Nick!" "Come, Nick!" etc.

Number One Lesson — House-training

If your puppy is less than three months old, do not expect any real results in house-training. You may try to paper-train him, but full physical control does not develop in some pups until they are six months old.

Paper-training

To paper-train, spread out newspapers in the area where you want the pup to go. Keep the papers separate from his sleeping quarters. He will not want to soil his own bed; therefore, he will use the paper. (At least that's the theory, but sometimes pups are not aware of our theories.) Put him on the paper when he first awakes, after every meal, and before bed. Every time he uses the newspaper reward him with the same kind word or a tidbit.

If you see your pup sniffing, circling, or squatting, take him quietly to the paper and pet him.

When your pup has an accident, don't rub his nose in the mess, and don't spank him. A firm "No!" perhaps accompanied by the loud swat of a rolled newspaper across your hand should be enough. All scoldings must directly follow the accident or the pup cannot make the connection.

All traces of his accident should be washed up with disinfectant or deodorizer. If the dog smells the soil he has made, he will repeat the error.

Paper-training works best with small breeds. If you have a large breed, you may wish to housebreak him outdoors right from the start.

Outside-training

Outside-training uses the same procedure as papertraining. Put your dog out early in the morning, after every meal, before retiring, and when you see him sniffing and circling around.

As long as he keeps off the sidewalks or the neighbor's lawn, let your dog nose around and pick his spot. The more often you are able to take your dog out, the sooner you will accomplish training. As soon as your dog has performed, praise him and take him back in. If he is allowed to play, he will forget the reason for having gone out.

Always keep your dog on a regular schedule. If you shift times, you may lose days of work. Gradually lengthen the time your dog must wait to go outside, but only by a few minutes each time. Remember, dogs want to be house-trained. With your encouragement and patience there should be no difficulty.

Don't let your dog get *too* set in his training. Let one person do all the house-training, but when the dog is fairly well along in his education, let someone else take him out. Also, vary the spot that he is expected to use, or he may resist using any other place.

If you are house-breaking a badly trained grown dog, don't be discouraged. He will be trained in time. Take him out regularly and praise him lavishly. You may want to leash him inside until taken out. He will be less likely to soil a spot where he knows he must remain.

Curb those bad habits— curb your dog

A careless dog usually means a careless owner. Whether you live in the city or the country, make sure your dog never leaves a mess on a sidewalk or lawn. If he makes a mess, it's your job to clean it up.

When you are anywhere but in your own yard, always edge your pup into the street if he wishes to evacuate. Most dogs can wait until they reach the street, and soon will, as a matter of habit.

Keeping Your Dog Quiet (And the Neighbors Happy)

High on the list of most-beloved dogs is the dog who knows when to bark and when not to.

While you do not wish your dog to stop barking entirely, especially if you expect him to act as a watchdog, you must restrain his barking if you want to keep your neighbors on speaking terms with you.

In general, small breeds tend to be barkers. Dogs bark more when confined. They are lonesome for you. Also, when they are left alone they have time to store up energy that must be worked, or barked, off.

If a dog is bored, the slightest noise — the telephone, the doorbell, a passing car — can set him off. Frequent exercise will very often solve the problem of the barking dog by letting him run off the frustration of confinement.

You can train a dog to stay alone for considerable periods of time without barking. If he is a puppy, he can learn this lesson easily. Put him in a room with some of his toys and say "Quiet!" Then leave, going far enough so he does not catch your scent. When whining or barking begins, return to him and once again say "Quiet!" or "No!" very firmly. You may demonstrate by holding his muzzle tightly shut. Repeat the lesson over and over, staying away for longer periods of time if the dog is quiet.

Older dogs will respond to this "no-bark" lesson, too. Your frequent returns reassure your dog that you will always come back.

However, if you are training an older dog, you may actually have to leave your home each time (and hope the neighbors don't think you're crazy!). Your dog will be keenly aware of your scent or any sounds you make if you remain in the house.

Silencing the overwatchful watchdog.

It is all well and good if your dog barks when strangers approach, but the dog who barks at regular callers should be reprimanded. You may have to introduce him to your friends and to the regular deliverymen. Then be on hand to censure him sharply if he is not friendly with those whose scents he should recognize.

If your dog's barking problem does not respond to your training efforts, you may be wise to turn to a professional handler for assistance. By no means should the noise be allowed to go on. No one loves a yapper.

Leash-training

Walking your dog can be a relaxing daily pleasure or an exhausting tug-of-war depending on how well you train your dog to accompany you on a leash. Almost all cities these days have a leash law, so not only is leash-walking your dog the only safe way, but it is also the only legal way to take your dog out.

The collar and leash

The best collar for training purposes is the chain-link slip collar. With this type of collar you can provide a sharp though painless correction to your dog's mistakes by jerking it. However, a heavy leather collar is advisable for long-haired dogs. The leash should be six feet long and of chain links or pliable leather, strong enough to restrain your dog at his strenuous best.

The training session

Set aside ten or fifteen minutes a day for your dog's training session. Choose a time when your dog is rested, and before he is fed. (He's more alert when he's hungry.) If possible, have the dog spend some time alone before you work with him. He'll be glad to see you then and more likely to respond well.

A dog will train more easily if you practice frequently and for short periods of time, never more than fifteen minutes at most. When he loses interest, give up for the time being.

Tidbit rewards are fine for some training, but

in the case of leash-walking, your dog should be expected to perform correctly without reward. Your approval should be enough.

Commands

The "heel" command and the other simple commands that follow may take ten days to two weeks to learn, and sometimes even longer. You can expect slips if you do not keep up the training.

Most pups resent even a collar, let alone a leash. When your pup has become used to his collar (be sure to let it out as he grows), put the leash on and let him drag it for a few minutes before you begin the lesson. Soothe the pup, but let him know by means of a gentle tug which way he is expected to go. The first time he is on the leash it is a good idea to pick up the pup and take him away from his usual abode — the kennel or house — then put him on the ground. The dog is more likely to move toward home, going "back to the barn," as it were, than to move farther away. Go with him, gradually correcting him. Soon he will come and go in the direction you desire. Unless you have had a great deal of experience training dogs, do not try to leash-train your pup before he is two months old.

"HEEL." The proper way for your dog to walk on a leash is for him to "heel," which means to walk at your left side, his head about even with your heels. Although you must start out by teaching him to heel on the leash, he should be able to heel without the leash when he has mastered this step. You will, however, never take off the leash where he cannot walk safely without it.

Place your dog on your left side and grasp the leash with your left hand, about three feet up from the collar. Loop the rest of the leash around your right hand. Start walking forward at a fast pace, saying "Heel!" Follow the command with the dog's name if you wish. Make your words clear and sharp. If the dog dashes forward, pull him up short and repeat the command "Heel!" each time he fails. Your control should be with the left hand.

Eventually, the dog will learn to follow you without signal and without leash. At the first sign of an error, take up the leash again. *Do not drag your dog at any time.* Be firm and insistent, and praise warmly when he heels well.

"TURN." Turning is actually a part of heeling. When you wish to turn, you must teach your dog

A Polite Dog Is A Popular Dog 43

to sense it and to follow you instead of his nose. Show your dog you are going to turn by slowing up. If you wish to turn left, slow up, then pivot on your left foot and swing your right foot forward. With your foot or knee, gently nudge your dog into turning. For a turn to the right, pivot on the right foot and bring the dog around with you by exerting pressure on the leash. When you start out in the new direction repeat the command to heel.

Continue to practice turns, alternating left and right. Once your dog understands your signal — a slowing or shortening of your step — he will move along smoothly with you. When he moves along well, remove the leash, attaching it again for more practice if he errs on the turns.

"SIT." At this command your dog should sit down, not up. "Sit" follows naturally after heeling. Hold the leash in your right hand, close to the dog's collar. When he is heeling beside you, stop and command "Sit!" in a firm voice. At the same time pull up on the leash and push his hindquarters down. The upward pull on the leash will keep his head raised so that he cannot lie down.

44 The Dog You Care For

Do not let him go immediately. It may take a few dozen tries before your dog obeys. Praise him happily each time he responds. Gradually, as your dog learns, less pressure and pull need be exerted, and finally none at all. When your dog understands the spoken command and has responded correctly a few dozen times, take the leash off and test him, putting the leash back on if he fails.

"STAY." "Stay" means your dog should remain stationary wherever he is. It is an important command; in some instances safety may depend on it. "Stay" follows the "Sit" command, and is sometimes coupled with it as "Sit-Stay."

With the leash attached to his collar, have your dog heel and sit. Follow with the command "Stay!" raising the palm of your hand toward the dog. Step off with your right foot and stand directly in front of him. If he starts to stand up, tell him "No!" sharply, put him back in the "Sit" position, and say "Stay!" Walk around him after you give the command; later back away. Repeat "Stay!" again and again, for the dog wants very much to follow you. Always be ready to correct him quickly when he moves.

Later on you will be able to leave the room, and your dog will stay still until you return. Start by staying away only a few moments. (You will never, of course, torture your dog by making him stay for hours at a time.) When you return to the room, praise your dog for behaving so well.

"COME." Start your dog's lessons on "Come" by running through what he already knows: "Heel,"

"Turn," "Sit," "Stay." These run-throughs give him confidence. When he has stayed for a few moments, walk out to the end of the leash and say "Come!" sharply, perhaps clapping your hands. Jerk the leash gently toward you. When the dog is directly in front of you, tell him to "Sit!" Repeat this many times, praising him when he comes to you on command. He must learn "Come" thoroughly and never disobey it.

"STAND." "Stand" is a minor command which is easy to teach your dog. While he is heeling, stop, press his head gently with your right hand, and say "Stand!" If he tries to move ahead, hold him back gently but firmly, or press against his nose. Praise him when he stands still, and work without the leash when he obeys well.

"DOWN." Put your dog in the "Sit" position, press gently down on the leash with your right foot, with enough force to pull the dog's head downward.

Stay down while raising your right hand to shoulder level in the "Down" signal. Eventually the dog will do "Down" on the command alone. To return the dog from "Down" to "Sit," jerk the leash up gently and say "Sit!"

Professional training

If you'd like professional help, a trainer can teach

your dog obedience in a very short time. Also, your community may have dog-training sessions at the local park or playground.

Obedience schools, which teach dogs the activities that will qualify them for dog shows, are becoming more and more popular. Many owners find it fun to work with a trained handler; often the problems of teaching the dogs to "Heel," "Sit," "Stay," etc., are made much easier by following his advice.

Fees for these schools are surprisingly low. Many of the classes are run not for professional purposes, but for people who want to improve the manners of their dogs and to meet other dog owners while doing so.

Your local humane society or SPCA can give you information on these schools.

Who Loves a Problem Dog?

Too many a master puts up year after year with his dog's misbehavior, shrugging his shoulders and saying, "Well, that's Bonzo!" Worse is the owner who pretends Bonzo's flubs are cute.

There is seldom a need to put up with a dog's bad habits. The well-fed, well-exercised dog, who gets his share of love and attention, usually behaves fairly well. If he has an annoying habit, in most cases a few weeks' work will break it.

Most bad habits in your dog can be cured with proper training — if you are patient enough. It takes much, much more patience to put up with the habit.

Some Typical Dog Problems

Car-chasing

The safest course to take when a dog chases cars is to confine him to the yard or keep him restrained on a leash. Car-chasing only becomes a problem in areas where dogs are not required to be confined.

To break your dog of car-chasing, tie a rope around his body (not his neck), leaving twenty to thirty feet of slack. Let him race after a car, and zap! When he comes to the end of the rope he will come to a fast halt, usually not on all fours. Be sure you hold on tight. Most dogs will get discouraged after the rope has thrown them a few times. If yours doesn't, tie a length of pipe to his harness, it may seem cruel to bruise his shins, but an accident with a car is much worse.

Some trainers favor shooting a water pistol in the dog's face when he goes after the car. If none of these methods works, tether him. And if he barks while being tethered, train him out of *this* bad habit (see page 37 on barking).

Eating dirt

Puppies and even an occasional older dog often will eat their own droppings or other kinds of "dirt." When this happens, do not punish the dog. First look for a dietary deficiency. Perhaps the dog is not getting enough to eat, or is not getting a balanced diet. Another possibility is that he has worms and is satisfying his abnormal hunger by eating everything at hand.

If your dog is well fed and worm-free, your best course is simply to remove all droppings immediately. The dog has no choice then but to forget this unattractive habit.

Biting

Some dogs, whether from nervousness or from need to work out frustrations, tend to be biters. Once a dog has become a biter, it is difficult to change him. The best you can do is be aware of situations which cause him to bite, and guard against them.

You must, of course, fence your property or leash your dog so that he will not have a chance to confront others. If he is shy or jumpy, warn others not to bother him.

Destroying household property
Most dogs can be trained to respect household items and furniture once they have grown up. But proper training begins in puppyhood. When you find your dog happily gnawing on the dining room

50 The Dog You Care For

table-leg, give him a strong "No!" and substitute another object, such as a bone, that he *may* chew on. Never give him an old or discarded object (such as an old shoe) to chew unless you are willing to let him gnaw on its newer replacement.

Do not leave the dog alone with the object he is out to destroy until you are sure he will not attack it again. Each time he returns to the object reprimand him with another "No!" Shut him in his crate or alone in another room, taking him out and trying him again and again until he gets the idea.

Dogfights

What happens when suddenly, after a few angry growls, you find your dog is involved in a serious dogfight? Don't think a polite command will break it up. Nor will a yank on the collar do much except assure you of a nipped wrist.

One of these measures can be quickly effective:

1. Grab the tail or hind legs of one of the dogs and heave him away.

2. Swat the dogs with a board or stick.
3. Douse them with a bucket of water or turn on the hose.

Wandering

Often a dog who is allowed to roam free may disappear for days at a time. If he is a male, it may be that he is in search of a female in heat. A female in heat often wanders, too. (But let's hope you're not letting her out!)

Some dogs wander because they are not getting enough to eat and the neighbors' garbage cans look tempting. But more often, those who stray feel a lack of affection. In many major cities there are laws restricting animals from roaming the streets. A wandering dog is not a suitable pet. He is usually destructive in the home.

If you think your dog may be lonely, bored, or

in need of companionship, spend more time with him. Play with him daily and try to avoid leaving him alone for any length of time. In many cases, increased attention and affection will cure the wanderlust.

The over-affectionate dog
 Many male dogs embarrass their owners by mounting the leg of a child or an adult. Females in season often rub against people who may not be responsive to this degree of affection. This is normal behavior, and usually your firm "No!" will stop it.

The female presents little problem since her seasons are only twice a year. You can help your male dog work off his excess energy by increasing the amount of exercise he takes.

Jumping up

The "Sit-Stay" command should take care of the over-enthusiastic greeting some dogs insist on giving. If your dog ignores the command, put your knee into his stomach and push him gently over, saying very firmly, "No!" Or, you may step lightly on his hind feet while saying "No!" Substitute an acceptable greeting such as shaking hands. You don't want to discourage his friendly attitude.

Digging up the garden

Dogs love to roll or dig in a freshly sown garden or lawn. If you are consistent with your "No!" every time he approaches, he will soon learn that it's "paws off." If not, show him you mean it by squirting him with a hose.

Commercial dog repellents will discourage your dog's attention to the garden if nothing else will.

3

The Dog You Care For Will Be Healthy

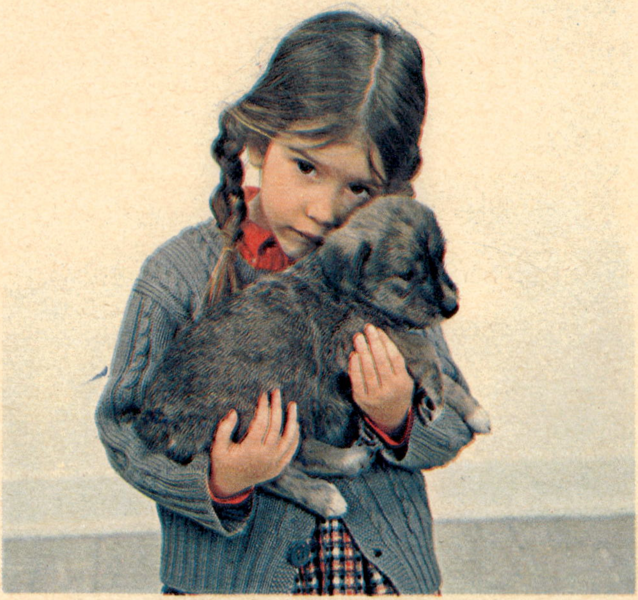

You don't want to take any chances with your dog's health. Since he can't tell you how he feels, you must keep a sharp lookout to be sure he's feeling his best.

Very soon after you get your dog you should have a veterinarian give him a thorough checkup (see page 23 to bring him up-to-date on the shots so necessary to every dog's good health.

Your Dog Should Have Four Shots

Distemper
Puppy shots should start two weeks after weaning, and be given until ten or eleven weeks, when adult shots are given. This vaccination, plus boosters as recommended by your veterinarian, is absolutely essential.

Hepatitis
This shot may be given in combination inoculation with distemper or administered separately.

Leptospirosis
Injection for both strains of this may be given alone or in combination with distemper and hepatitis injections.

Rabies
Vaccination is necessary at four to six months, followed by yearly boosters. This inoculation is required by law. Regulations concerning kind and frequency of booster shots vary by state.

58 The Dog You Care For

External Parasites

There are four external parasites which can make life miserable for your dog: fleas, lice, mites, and ticks. They are much too tiny for your dog to dislodge, although he'll never give up trying.

These parasites, besides being uncomfortable, carry disease. Fleas may carry tapeworm eggs. Ticks may carry blood parasites. Lice suck the dog's blood, and, in great numbers, can cause anemia. Mites cause mange. All parasites multiply incredibly fast.

You will know your dog has one of these four parasites when you see him scratching furiously and biting into his coat. But you may not know which parasite is causing the problem. In general, it is best to let your veterinarian identify the troublemaker and prescribe the proper powder, dip, or spray.

Commercial flea powders with 5 to 10 percent DDT are effective for fleas, lice, and ticks if dusted down to the skin. An aerosol spray makes it easier for you to get the medication all through the dog's coat, but you must be careful to keep the spray away from his eyes.

Be sure any preparation you use is safe for dogs. DDT preparations are unsafe for puppies or nursing dams. Most doggy powders and sprays are unsafe for cats, so *don't* use them on your feline too.

It is very important for you to eliminate the source of the parasite by cleaning out the dog's kennel, spraying it, and laundering his bedding. Bushes and trees in your dog's yard should be sprayed with a nontoxic insecticide so that parasites do not gather there.

Regular combing, brushing, stripping, and sponging with a residual solution will help remove parasites before they become firmly entrenched.

Internal Parasites

Perhaps half the dogs in this country have worms at one time or another. If your dog is a puppy, have him examined for worms, even though he may show no symptoms.

You may suspect that your dog has worms when you notice the following signs:

- He seems weak and listless.
- His appetite changes; he may stuff himself, or he may eat very little.
- He has diarrhea.
- His coat is poor.

You may actually see worms in his vomit and feces. When you suspect or discover worms, take a sample of the dog's stool to the veterinarian. He will treat your dog according to the type of parasite he has.

All worming should be done by a veterinarian or under his direction. Give a dog a patent medicine only if you know the type of worm he has or if you cannot consult a veterinarian. If you do use a patent medicine, be sure to follow directions to the letter.

Until worms are eliminated, give your dog a bland diet of cooked carbohydrates. Avoid raw meat and raw vegetables. For the dog's protection and yours, keep his living quarters clean. Use disinfectant on the floor. Change his drinking water often. Disinfect all feeding dishes and be sure to *rinse off all traces of disinfectant.*

Be sure to bury all droppings and to soak the dog's running area with a solution of borax and water, or salt and water. Worms are persistent; you need to be persistent too. Continue treatment until you are sure your dog is completely rid of the problem. These infestations seldom leave any lasting effects if treated promptly and completely.

Skin Disorders

Daily care for your pet's coat will go a long way toward helping him avoid the many and varied diseases which affect a dog's skin.

Because many skin disorders have symptoms in common, do not try to diagnose your dog's ailment and treat it. You may make matters worse. Whenever you see worn patches on the coat, pimples, inflammation, or rash, take your dog to the veterinarian. He can diagnose the exact nature of the disease. The cause can be any one of a number of things: external parasites, allergy, mange, impetigo — to mention only a few.

When Your Dog Is Ill

A dog that is ill deserves the same amount of care and concern as any other member of the family. Some dog owners seem to feel that nature will take

The Dog You Care For Will Be Healthy 61

care of the problem. Often nature will, but not without some needless suffering for the dog.

When you see that your dog is suffering, make him as comfortable as possible. It may not, however, be right for you to give him a remedy that was meant for people. Some of these remedies can be very harmful.

Don't take chances; put your mind at ease by calling your veterinarian right away. If the illness occurs after office hours and you do not have your veterinarian's home telephone number (it is wise to keep this handy at all times), look in the yellow pages and see if there is an emergency veterinary service listed. Many cities provide one.

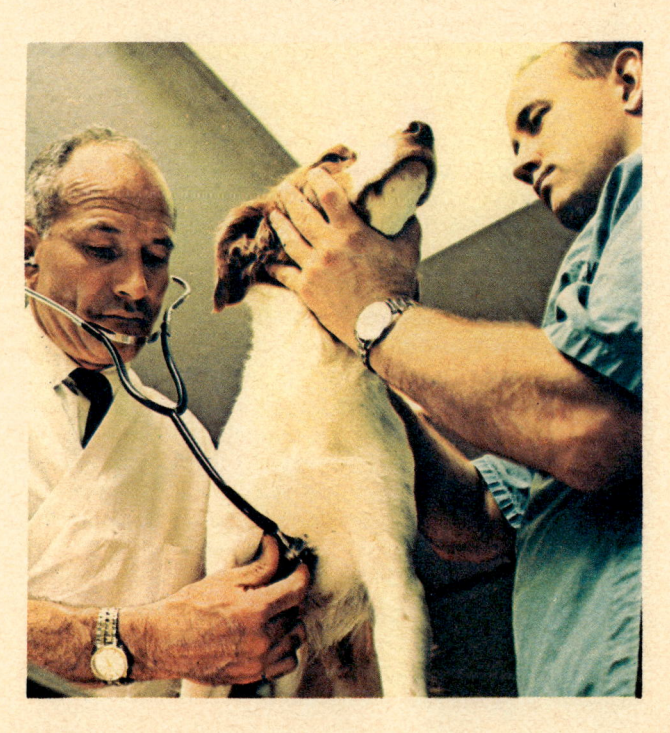

(Some veterinarians recommend an annual physical checkup for your dog whether he is ill or not.)

How do you know when he's ill?

Among veterinarians and breeders, the term "thrifty" indicates a vibrant or lively dog, and "unthrifty" the listless, lazy dog. When ill, your dog will lose his pep, his coat may lose its gloss, and his eyes will lose their gleam. He may be indifferent to food, and may have diarrhea or constipation. His tongue will be coated, his eyes runny. His nose may or may not be cold. (Contrary to belief, temperature of a dog's nose is no sure sign of health or disease.)

Taking his temperature

This is not difficult, and your dog will not mind it. Use an ordinary rectal thermometer, lubricated with vaseline. Insert half its length into the dog's rectum for two minutes. Average temperature is 101.5°, varying to 102° for small breeds.

Caring for the sick dog

If your family life is already overly busy, it is probably best to leave the sick dog in the hospital for treatment. Caring for him would take a great deal of time as well as love. However, if yours is a dog who will whine for his master, he will probably recuperate faster at home.

Your dog needs rest when he is ill, but like a little child, he often does not have the sense to stay quiet. It is up to you to restrict his activity. Put him in an isolated room or corner where it is warm and not drafty (about 70° is best). If the weather is bad, you may not want him to go outside. Put newspapers in the area where he is convalescing. Make sure his room is not too sunny; some illnesses make a dog's eyes sensitive to light.

Keep a daily check on temperature, breathing,

bowel movements, appetite, urination, nasal discharge, and vomiting to help you accurately describe your dog's progress to your veterinarian.

Keeping the patient clean

If your dog is well enough to go outdoors to evacuate, or can use the newspapers in his sickroom, your problem is not difficult. If your dog goes outdoors, be sure that you wipe off his feet when he returns so that he will not bring dirt back to his sickbed.

If he is too weak to get up, cover the bed with easily washable small towels or clean paper. A small towel can also serve as a diaper if necessary. Wipe him often with a soft cloth moistened with mild antiseptic and dust him with talc. (Take care that the talc is not inhaled.) If he is paralyzed or so weakened that he cannot move easily, turn him over often to prevent bedsores.

Long-haired dogs who are immobilized for any length of time should be clipped around the hindquarters and other contact areas.

Administering medicines

Follow precisely all directions for administering medicines. If your veterinarian prescribes medication for certain times, you cannot skip one time and give a double dose the next.

If the dog's medicine is not bad-tasting you may be able to administer it easily by mixing it with food or liquids that he likes. But your dog's very intelligent nose may at once detect that foreign scent in his food.

If your dog won't take medicine with his food and won't open his mouth and swallow it willingly, here is what you must do:

PILLS. Butter the pill to make it slippery. Grasp dog's muzzle, squeeze lips against teeth, apply pressure just forward of the corners of his mouth. Push lips between teeth. (If he gets rough he will bite himself.) Tilt head backward. Place, don't throw, tablet toward base of tongue. Close his mouth firmly, then massage his throat, lifting muzzle up. The dog will have no choice but to swallow.

LIQUIDS. Grasp dog's lower lip in front of the corner of his mouth and pull it out gently to form a pouch. Pour medicine (preferably from a small bottle), a little at a time, then close the pouch and let the dog swallow. If you lift his muzzle up, he has little choice but to let the medicine run through his clenched teeth and down his throat.

Be firm, but kind and gentle. The dog will soon see that you mean business and that it is useless to resist.

Warning: Do not throw either liquids or pills down the dog's throat. They could enter the windpipe and cause serious trouble.

Caring for the Old Dog

A six-month-old puppy may be compared with a child of six years. The year-old dog is like a youth of fifteen. After two years, each single year equals four years in man. So if your dog is fifteen years old, he is a senior citizen past seventy in dogdom. Large dogs usually grow old faster than small ones.

As your dog approaches old age, he will need frequent checkups if his life is to be prolonged. Each year will lessen his ability to resist disease, and ailments of the aged will threaten him.

Watch him carefully to see that he does not overtax himself or overeat. Remember, he can no longer exercise as he formerly did. You should be on the lookout for impaired eyesight and hearing, which will put him in danger if he is allowed to roam free.

Constipation from lack of activity is a frequent complaint of the older dog. You may have to give him a mild laxative or stool softener frequently (see page 70 on constipation) and adjust his diet (see page 96, Feeding the Older Dog).

Your Dog's Medicine Cabinet and First-aid Kit

To be prepared for illness or accident, your dog's medicine cabinet should include the following:
1. Sterile cotton
2. Pain-relieving ointment, such as Nupercainal
3. Mustard powder, hydrogen peroxide, or salt (emetics)
4. Tannic-acid ointment or other burn ointment
5. Adhesive tape and bandages
6. Antiseptic, such as Metaphen, for dressing wounds
7. Blunt-ended scissors
8. Activated charcoal (antidote for all poisonings)
9. Snake serum, razor blades (in snake country)
10. Aromatic spirits of ammonia (for shock)

Other important aids
1. Rectal thermometer
2. Vaseline
3. Mineral oil or milk of magnesia (laxatives)
4. Kaopectate (for diarrhea)
5. Rubbing alcohol (a disinfectant)
6. Aspirin
7. Dramamine or Bonamine (for car sickness)
8. Tweezers
9. Flea and lice powder or spray
10. Mercuric oxide for eye irritations
11. Germicidal soap (tincture of green soap for poison ivy)

Except for the medicines listed above, do not put any preparations in your dog's medicine cabinet that are not intended specifically for dogs. Scale down the dosage of the above-mentioned internal medicines to your dog's weight. For instance, aver-

66 The Dog You Care For

age human dosage for a 150-pound person would have to be cut to one-fifth to suit a 20- to 30-pound terrier.

When Your Dog Is Injured

If your dog meets with an accident, there are many ways you can help him before the veterinarian can treat him. Do not depend too much on your first aid, however. If the dog is badly hurt, the veterinarian should be consulted right away.

A few points to remember in case of accident:
- Stop all bleeding immediately.
- Do not change the dog's position.

- Make sure the dog is warm; shock usually accompanies an accident.
- Do not give water — the injury may be internal.

Restraint

Injured dogs often need to be restrained before first aid can be administered. A dog in severe pain may even turn on his master.

Make a *mouth tie* from a large loop of strong cloth, cord, or old nylon stocking and slip it over the dog's nose. Make sure his nostrils are free. Pull the loop tight and run the ends under his ears so that you can tie them behind his head.

If the dog starts to vomit, remove this muzzle immediately or he may choke to death. Tie the dog to a tree or pole if he tries to run away.

Artificial respiration

If the dog is not breathing, the best method of resuscitation (though one of the most difficult) is to apply mouth-to-mouth breathing. Cup your hands into a cone and breathe directly into the dog's mouth and nostrils until he starts to breathe on his own.

The other method of artificial respiration is also similar to that given to people. Place the dog on his right side, with his head and neck extended. Draw his tongue forward. Press with sudden but gentle movement over the dog's ribs, behind the shoulder blade. After this sudden movement, relax immediately. Count to five, then start again. Press and release about twenty to thirty times per minute until the dog begins to breathe. The rhythm must be smooth and regular.

When the dog is breathing, treat him for shock (see page 74).

The first-aid chart that follows may be referred to quickly in emergencies.

FIRST-AID CHART

Type of Injury or Illness	Things to Do	Things to Avoid
Abrasions	Apply restraint. Clip hair around wound. Wash with mild soap and warm water. Apply boric acid or other mild antiseptic.	
Automobile accident	Call the veterinarian. Apply restraint. Check bleeding. Apply tourniquet between cut and heart if there is arterial bleeding (spurting). Cover with blanket.	Don't move the dog. Don't give him water.
Bee stings	Apply mouth tie. Apply cold compress. Apply warm compress if swelling is severe. Apply painkilling ointment such as Nupercainal. If dog appears faint, take to veterinarian.	

Bruises	Apply cold compress and bandage to bruised part to limit area of swelling.	
Burns: chemical	Apply alkaline solution of 1 pt. warm water and 1 tbsp. baking soda or washing soda, or wash with milk of magnesia. Apply tannic-acid jelly or concentrated cool tea. Take to veterinarian.	
Burns: extensive (when one-quarter or more of the dog's skin is affected)	Call veterinarian. Treat for shock. Cover with clean, *dry* dressing.	Do not apply any greases, ointments, or other first-aid burn remedies.
Burns: small or superficial	Apply ice cubes, or *cold* water. Cut away hair. Apply burn ointment	
Cat or dog bites	Apply mouth tie. Let wounds stay open to bleed. Insert cotton-tipped toothpicks with antiseptic into wounds. Take to veterinarian for shot.	

FIRST-AID CHART (continued)

Type of Injury or Illness	Things to Do	Things to Avoid
Constipation	Give milk of magnesia, 1 tsp. for every 10 lbs. of body weight.	Do not give any other laxatives intended for people. Do not give laxative if you suspect trouble is caused by swallowed object.
Convulsions (Symptoms: Chattering of jaws, foaming at mouth, rapid breathing, dog lies on side "paddling.")	Keep dog leashed. See veterinarian.	
Cuts, tears, punctures	Apply restraint. Remove object causing wound. Control bleeding. Cover wound with sterile gauze soaked in antiseptic.	

Diarrhea	Give Kaopectate, 1 tsp. per 10 lbs. of dog. Feed cooked starches. Watch for other symptoms.	Do not give fluid foods like milk or broth.
Drowning	Hold dog up by hind legs to drain water from breathing passages. Apply artificial respiration (see page 67). Dry and treat for shock.	
Electric shock	Unplug wire or push dog away from wire with stick. Treat for shock. Give artificial respiration if necessary (see page 67).	Don't touch dog, unless you are wearing rubber gloves, until wire is detached from him.
Eye injury	Wash with mild solution of salt water. Keep eye moist. Call veterinarian if injury seems serious.	

FIRST-AID CHART (continued)

Type of Injury or Illness	Things to Do	Things to Avoid
Fracture	Call veterinarian. Apply restraint. Keep warm, treat for shock. Immobilize limb with splint if you cannot reach the veterinarian. Give aspirin (½ a 5 gr. tablet per 30 lbs.).	
Frostbite	Take dog to warm place for gradual thawing.	Do not rub with snow or ice.
Indigestion	Give milk of magnesia, 1 tsp. for every 10 lbs. of body weight.	
Objects in mouth and throat	Force mouth open by pressing cheeks. Call veterinarian immediately if object cannot be removed.	Don't give emetic if sharp object has been swallowed.

Poisoning
(Symptoms: Trembling, abdominal pain, drooling, convulsions, shallow breathing, eventual coma.)

Call veterinarian.
Give an emetic, such as hydrogen peroxide mixed equally with water, or 2 tsp. salt in a cup of warm water, or 1 tbsp. mustard powder in warm water.
Give antidote as listed on container or give activated charcoal, 3 or 4 tbsp. in warm water.

If corrosive poison, give no emetic.

Poison ivy

Wearing rubber gloves, wash dog with brown laundry soap or tincture of green soap. Poison ivy will probably not affect dog, only persons who touch poison on coat.

Porcupine quills

If a few quills, apply mouth tie, cut quills with scissors, ease out carefully with tweezers or needle-nose pliers.
Treat as for puncture wounds.
Or take dog to veterinarian immediately for removal under anesthetic.

FIRST-AID CHART (continued)

Type of Injury or Illness	Things to Do	Things to Avoid
Shock (Symptoms: Gums look whitish, pulse is feeble and rapid, breathing shallow.)	Lower dog's head. Keep him warm and quiet. Let him sniff spirits of ammonia.	Don't give whiskey. Don't give fluids if internal injuries may be present.
Skunk odor	Wash eyes with salt-water solution of ½ tsp. salt to ½ glass warm water. Apply eye ointment. Wash dog in tomato juice, followed by soap and water, then 5% solution of ammonia.	
Snake bite	Apply tourniquet. Rush to veterinarian for antivenom shot. Or slash wound with an X, squeeze out blood. Suck wound with snake-bite suction cup, or your mouth (if your mouth has no cuts or sores). Wash with full-strength hydrogen peroxide. Carry to veterinarian.	Do not let dog walk.

Sprain	Treat for fracture, as you may not be able to tell the difference between a sprain and fracture.	
Suffocation	Give artificial respiration (see page 67). Treat for shock.	Do not force liquids; give them only if he can swallow.
Sunstroke or heatstroke (Symptoms: Rapid breathing, loud panting, vomiting, rapid pulse, staggering, inability to focus.)	Place in shade. Sponge with cool water or give shallow cold bath. Cover with towel which has been soaked in cold water.	
Unconsciousness (from concussion or stroke)	Call veterinarian. Keep warm and quiet.	Do not give stimulants.

4

Grooming Is A Part Of Good Health

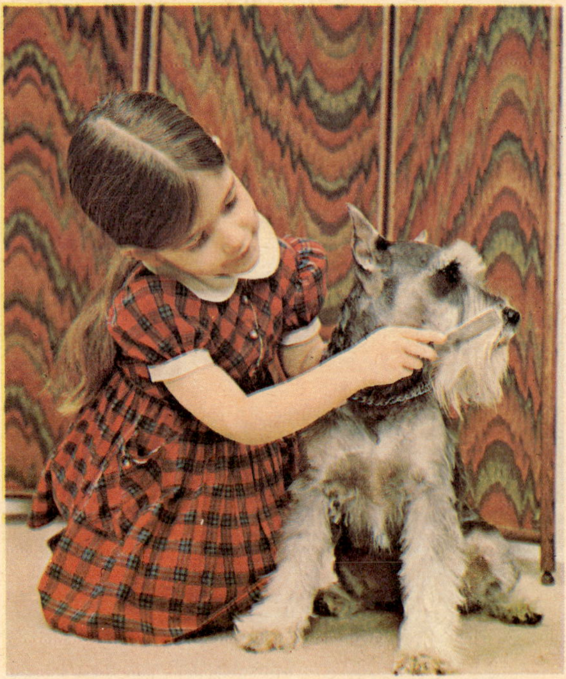

You will want your dog to be the handsomest animal you know how to make him. Even a dog of mixed breeds can be a beautiful animal if he is healthy and well cared for.

As you learned from the previous chapter, good grooming is actually a part of your dog's health. An ungroomed dog can suffer unnecessarily from fleas and lice, from mange caused by mites, from skin diseases, from heat, from matted hair in the intestine. All dogs need regular combing and/or brushing, regardless of the length of hair, but long-haired dogs need to be groomed daily.

Your Dog's Grooming Kit

Every well-groomed dog should own the following:

- Short- or long-bristled brush, depending on length of coat.
- Comb with wide teeth for long-haired or wire-haired dog.
- Stripping knife for wire-haired dogs; wool comb for long-haired dogs.
- Scissors (barber type).
- Nail clippers.

Giving Him a Handsome Coat

Proper grooming takes only a few minutes a day. For short-haired dogs a brush is sufficient. With medium- or long-haired dogs begin with the comb. Work rapidly but gently, reassuring your dog with a few kind words. Divide and cut out matted hair with scissors pointed away from dog. Remove burrs. Then *brush* in the direction you want the hair to lie. The comb has done most of the work, but both comb and brush are necessary for a glossy, clean coat.

In summer, keep the dog's coat free of dead hair by removing it with a stripping knife or wool comb instead of cutting the hair short. In hot weather you should do this every day, followed by regular combing and brushing to prevent your pet from shedding his coat everywhere. Regular combing, brushing, and stripping will also help to eliminate parasites before they get a firm hold.

Do not clip your dog's coat in the summer. Short prickly hairs may make him itchy and miserable. With certain breeds such as the poodle a special style of haircut in the summer is all right. This type of clipping and trimming should usually be left to the experienced or professional groomer.

Nails

Your dog may be very uncomfortable if his nails are not kept trimmed. How often you trim the nails depends on how much time your dog spends on cement or pavement and how frequent his exercise is. Puppies, apartment dogs, and older dogs need nails trimmed more often.

The first time you trim your dog's nails play safe — use a mouth restraint, even though he may not mind the clipping at all. Use clippers made for animals, of the correct size for your breed of dog. Cut only the tip, or transparent part, of the nail. Cut a little bit at a time. Be especially careful with black nails — you cannot see the quick. Do not forget the dewclaw nail if it was not removed when the dog was a puppy. It is advisable to have your veterinarian show you how to trim the dog's nails when you take him in for his first checkup.

Eyes

If your dog's eyes have become irritated from dust or a foreign object, flush them out with a mild salt-water solution.

Ears

Clean your dog's ears as part of his regular grooming routine. Do not wash them; they should be cleansed with baby oil. Do not poke or probe or stretch the tissue. Reassure your dog — his ears are very sensitive.

Teeth

Tartar deposits are often the cause of bad breath in dogs. If there is a heavy accumulation, have your veterinarian scale it off. An occasional large bone will help remove tartar, too.

Bathing

If your dog has been groomed daily and has occasional sponge baths followed by a rubdown, he will need a bath very infrequently. Doggy odor usually disappears with thorough daily grooming.

When you do bathe your dog, be sure the room is free of drafts. Put cotton in your dog's ears (don't forget to remove it) and mineral oil in the corner of each eye to protect him from suds. Wash him in warm, not hot, water, using a mild soap or detergent. Remove soap completely (a tablespoon of vinegar in the rinse water will help); if the lather is not washed away it can irritate his skin. Dry your dog thoroughly and keep him inside for at least an hour.

Treat your dog like a "show" dog. You will be rewarded for the small amount of time you spend each day grooming him. You'll discover that he has become a handsome pet, and you'll feel you have a dog you can "show" proudly to your friends. However, it isn't your dog's vanity that you are really concerned with, but his comfort and his health.

5

A Well-Fed Dog Is A Healthy Dog

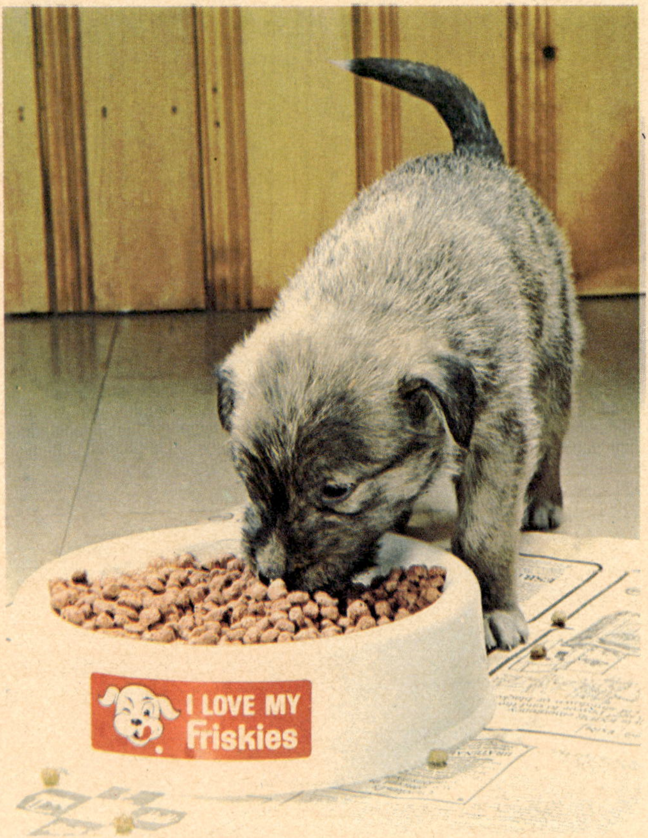
I LOVE MY
Friskies

THE best way to keep your dog healthy is to keep him well fed. Well fed, however, does not mean overfed. Many owners, worried that their dog will not be properly nourished, actually feed them too much. Overeating, especially of the wrong foods, can do more harm than eating too little.

Some Common Food Fallacies

People have been so overanxious about nutrition for their pets that a number of feeding fallacies have grown up through the years. It has only been through scientific research over the last thirty years or so that these misconceptions have been corrected and the true facts about good dog nutrition brought to light. Here are answers to some common errors that have been misleading dog owners for years:

Is lean meat the most important part of a good diet for dogs? No. The person who relies on lean meat as the mainstay of the dog's diet can do his pet much harm by not giving him the balanced nourishment he needs. Meats in the dog's diet should not be lean — dogs need fats for energy, healthy skin, growth, and resistance.

Will raw meat make a dog wild or vicious? There is no basis for this belief. A diet of raw meat alone, however, could make your animal irritable and ill if his diet lacks other essential elements.

Is starch indigestible for dogs? While raw starches are not digested by a dog's system, cooked starch should be part of every dog's diet. It provides carbohydrates the dog needs for energy and bulk.

Can raw meat or milk cause worms? Not necessarily. Worms come only from worm eggs, which are not found in milk or U.S. inspected raw meat. Your dog should not eat freshly killed animals he or a hunter has caught — they might contain tapeworm. Pork should always be cooked to avoid trichinosis.

Will sulphur, garlic, or raw onions cure worms? No. Worm medicine is the only remedy your dog can take that is strong enough to kill worms.

Will raw eggs keep the coat shiny? Raw egg per se will do nothing for the coat. Egg yolk might contribute to a totally balanced diet, but a totally balanced diet need not necessarily contain *raw* egg yolk. Raw white of egg is actually harmful because it interferes with absorption of biotin, an important vitamin. Cooking of the whole egg destroys the harmful factor in the egg white.

Do dogs need to chew on bones? Although bones are not necessary for a dog, he does enjoy one now and then, and it may help clean tartar off his teeth. The bone you give him must be a heavy knuckle or shank bone, never a sharp chop, spare rib, poultry, or rabbit bone, all of which can splinter.

Will bolting food cause indigestion? No. Your dog's digestive system is adapted to an eat-and-run feeding, probably a carry-over from primitive days. When you see your dog bolt his food, be glad he's enjoying it.

Do purebreds require a special diet? Not at all. A good balanced diet is the same for all breeds; only the amount varies. (See chart, page 91.)

Do fresh foods provide a better diet than canned or dried dog foods? The opposite is often the case. Many a dog owner who goes to the trouble and expense of planning a fresh diet for his dog — such as raw meat, eggs, and fish — leaves out important vitamins and minerals, fats, and carbohydrates provided by quality commercial dog foods, and his dog suffers for all his trouble.

Doesn't a dog need variety to maintain his appetite? He does not. While some dogs enjoy several flavors — such as chicken, liver, or beef — others prefer to stay with one favorite only. There is no need for a wide variety in the diet. Once you have found a balanced diet that your dog enjoys stick with it. Changes in brands and/or types of prepared foods should be made gradually and carefully so that the dog's system is not upset. You must be sure, however, that the steady diet you have chosen for your dog is balanced, or eventually you will see signs of deficiency: lack of energy, poor coat, lowered resistance to disease.

Feeding Your Dog a Balanced Diet — The Easy Way

It would be difficult for the most conscientious dog lover (unless he is a professional nutritionist) to procure and prepare day after day a diet that contains protein, carbohydrates, fats, vitamins, and minerals in the correct proportions. That is why most dog owners are advised to let their pet's nutrition be planned by the experts who formulate the diets for quality commercial pet foods.

88 The Dog You Care For

Today, thanks to the extensive scientific research made possible by Friskies' up-to-date facilities, you are guaranteed a totally balanced diet for your dog when you choose any one of the Friskies foods to feed him.

Constant research by Friskies

Scientists at Carnation Research Laboratories in Van Nuys, California, and at Friskies Nutrition Research Kennels at Carnation Farms, Carnation, Washington, work together, constantly testing and improving nutrition for your dog or cat. Their more than thirty years of experience assure your pet the very best that modern nutritional science can provide.

Many dogs at the Friskies Kennels, which breed for the highest standards, have been maintained in perfect health their entire lives on Friskies foods alone — proof of Friskies fully-balanced complete nourishment.

Ch. Bardene Bingo, a Scottish terrier, best-in-show winner at the ninety-first Westminster Dog Show at Madison Square Garden — the top honor in dogdom — is a Friskies dog, owned by Carnation Farms.

You can feed your dog any one or all of these nourishing products which will help to maintain him in a healthy condition. These types of dog food give him all the variety he wants.

Carnation Farms, Carnation, Washington (photo courtesy of Carnation Company)

Top dog Ch. Bardene Bingo from Friskies Kennels (photo courtesy of Carnation Company)

- Friskies canned dog foods, in five flavors
- Friskies Dinners
- Friskies Sauce Cubes

And for the puppy under one year, there is Friskies Puppy Food.

The How and When of Feeding

Whatever time of day you decide to feed your dog, keep to the same hour to avoid upsetting his system. Actually, a grown dog need only be fed once a day. It is usually preferable to feed him in the evening, before your own meal. This will discourage him from begging table scraps that can throw his diet off balance or cause him to overeat. Also, a full, satisfying meal given to your dog in the evening will help him settle for the night.

If you feel he needs it, you may give your dog the smaller part of his ration in the morning. Do not feed him directly after exercising.

If you mix your dog's dry food with water or milk, serve it fresh each feeding. Keep canned food under refrigeration once it has been opened. If your dog does not eat his food, don't leave it out for an extended length of time; remove it and give him fresh food the next mealtime. Don't try to tempt a lagging appetite with special tidbits or you may find yourself with a finicky eater. Your dog will not starve himself, and an occasional missed meal is natural.

The self-feeding method

This method of feeding is convenient if your dog likes his food dry. Dry foods can be left out without spoiling — so the dog can nibble whenever he wants, and the owner can be away at mealtime. Do not start self-feeding when your dog is very hungry, or he may gorge himself. Whenever you feed him dry food, be sure to furnish plenty of fresh water.

Modified diets for special cases

For hard-working dogs, such as hunting dogs, or for a whelping female, the Friskies diet has only to be increased in quantity to take care of the extra stress. For puppies and small breeds, Friskies makes a special product, Friskies Puppy Food. Consult your veterinarian if you have a particular problem which may require a prescription diet.

Water

Fresh cool water should be available at all times. A dog on a dry or soft-moist diet will require more water than the dog who eats canned food.

You will find the following chart handy as an approximate guide to how much your dog should eat. Remember, though, only you can be the judge of how much your dog needs. Amounts vary according to your dog's age, activity, physiology, and temperament.

Feeding Chart

Amounts of dry Friskies to feed

To meet the average dog's calorie and protein requirements for proper nutrition, feed from one-third ounce (large dogs) to one-half ounce (small dogs) of dry dog food for each pound the dog weighs. A common measuring cup holds approximately three ounces of dry dog food. Never feed more than your dog eats readily.

Note: Hard-working dogs and pregnant or nursing females require considerably larger quantities in proportion to size and activity. Feed larger dogs in proportion. Supply the following amounts daily in one or two feedings as you prefer (amounts listed are dry measure):

Typical Breed	Dog's Weight	Amount of Dry Dog Food
Setter, Collie	75 lbs.	9 cups
	50 lbs.	6 cups
Spaniel, Airedale	40 lbs.	5 cups
	30 lbs.	4 cups
Cocker, Terrier	25 lbs.	3 cups
	15 lbs.	2 cups
Toy Breeds	12 lbs.	1 3/4 cups
	6 lbs.	1 1/4 cups

92 The Dog You Care For

Amounts of canned Friskies to feed

Feed Friskies Meat, Liver, Chicken, Kidney and Bacon or Lamb Flavor canned food at room temperature once or twice a day according to dog's size, condition, and activity. For a moderately active dog, allow about three-quarters of an ounce of food per pound of his weight.

For variety, Friskies canned dog food may be alternated or mixed with Friskies Dinners or Friskies Sauce Cubes.

Feeding Your Puppy

Those lively little puppies move so fast (and grow so fast) that they need to be fed often. Friskies Puppy Food (thoroughly mixed with one and one-half parts of warm water or milk to one part of Puppy Food) can be given to pups at weaning time (three to six weeks of age) and they will dig into it eagerly. (Warm water brings out flavor and odor of the food.)

A Well-Fed Dog Is A Healthy Dog

Right after weaning, pups need to be fed four or five times a day at regular intervals. Gradually decrease moisture added to the Puppy Food until you are mixing it two parts Puppy Food to one part warm water. The number of feedings should be reduced gradually to two feedings a day at the age of six months.

As soon as the pup can handle them, usually at about nine months, you may wish to feed him Friskies Sauce Cubes to give his jaws and teeth some healthy chewing (which a puppy loves). Pour hot water over them to bring out the meaty flavor. They make their own gravy. At approximately one year old, a dog will have reached maturity and may be fed an exclusive diet of Friskies Dinners and/or Sauce Cubes.

Put out only the amount of moistened Dinner or Sauce Cubes that can be consumed in a reasonably short period of time (say a half hour); then take up the dish and wash it thoroughly. If there is any food left over, it can be reserved several hours in a tightly covered dish.

PUPPY FEEDING SCHEDULE

Age of Puppy	Number of Meals per Day	Food/Preparation	Amounts to Feed
☐ **3 - 4 Weeks** Puppies actively nursing are supplemented with a moist, liquid gruel of Friskies Puppy Food.	**1 to 2** Start with one feeding a day, increase to two feedings by the 4th week.	Make a gruel at the ratio of 1 cup* warm water, milk or broth to 1 cup* Friskies Puppy Food. Reduce water every day from 4th to 5th week so that food is more solid rather than a gruel. water [cup] + [cup] Puppy Food	3/4 oz. dry Friskies Puppy Food per 1 lb. body weight.
☐ **5 - 7 Weeks** Mother stays away for longer periods, allowing increased number of supplemental meals per day.	**2 to 3**	From 5 weeks on, feed at the ratio of 1 cup warm water to 2 cups Friskies Puppy Food. Same moist texture and consistency as adult ration. [cup] + [cup] water Puppy Food	Puppies vary. Any feeding guide as to amounts should be followed only so far as common sense dictates. Below is the total daily requirement of the average puppy from the age of 5 weeks on. Amounts should be split into the number of meals on puppy's daily schedule. Puppy's Weight Daily amounts of Dry Friskies Puppy Food

☐ **7 Weeks - 3 Months** Puppies completely weaned.	**3 to 4** Where convenient, the 4th feeding can be a "go to bed" treat.	*See above*	5 to 8# 1 to 2 cups 8 to 10# 2 to 3 cups 10 to 15# 3 to 4 cups 15 to 20# 4 to 5 cups 20 to 25# 5 to 6 cups *See Chart above*
☐ **3 to 6 Months** Fast growing period.	**3**	*See above*	*See Chart above* Steadily increase amount fed, particularly in the fast-growing, larger breeds. During this period many pups double their weight in as little as 2 to 3 weeks, so it is wise to feed them all they will eat, to make sure they are not underfed.
☐ **6 to 12 Months** Puppies have gained greater capacity and are leveling out in their growth rate.	**2**	*See above* *1 cup = 8 oz. water or 3½ oz. Dry Friskies Puppy Food.	*See Chart above*

95

Feeding the Older Dog

The older dog should eat less than he did during his young maturity because he now is less active. You may have to give him two or three small feedings a day. His appetite often lags, and he is unenthusiastic about a large meal. You may add a few treats now and then to keep him interested. Be careful to keep his feeding times regular; he is very sensitive to changes in routine.

If your aging dog appears not to be getting full benefit from his food, consult your veterinarian. He may need a geriatric supplement added to his daily fare.

6

To Mate Or Not To Mate

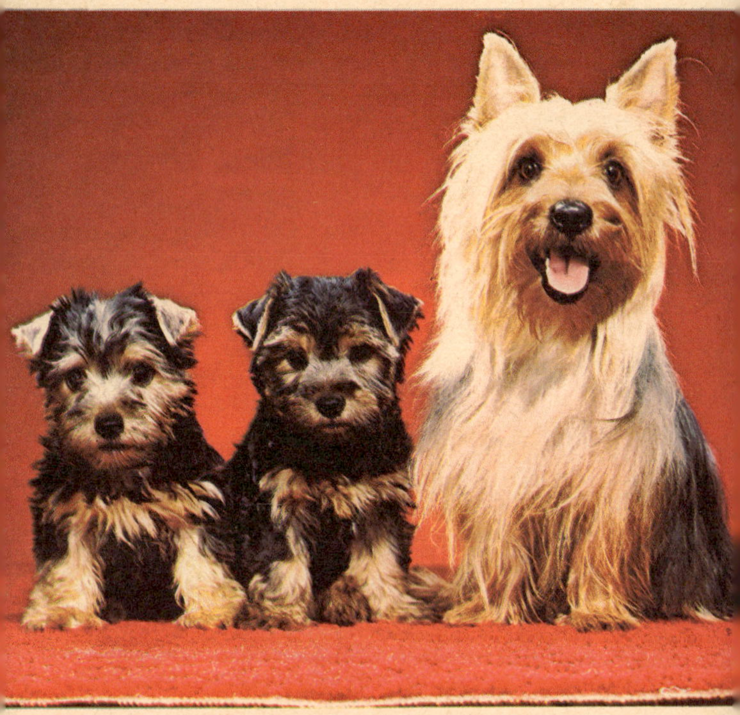

The Female's Season

If your dog is a female ("bitch" is the correct term), she will have reached sexual maturity and had her first season sometime between her sixth and tenth month. After this she will usually come into heat at regular six-month intervals.

You will know when your female is coming into heat by these signs: She will become restless and lose her appetite, and her vulva will become swollen. She will have a slight discharge or bleeding for four to seven days.

When this discharge tapers off, she is receptive to male dogs for three to five days — sometime during the second week after heat has started. The best time for her to mate is generally between the tenth to fourteenth day from the onset of heat. After this she will suddenly reject masculine attention, and you know her season is ending.

Confining the female

During her season you must confine your female if you do not want a litter of puppies. Neighborhood dogs will quickly pick up the scent of a bitch in season, and you may be bothered to death with male callers.

Your veterinarian may give you some pills which will decrease the attractive scent of your female, or you may find it convenient to place her in a kennel during this time. If you cannot do this, keep her indoors until her season is over. (This will be approximately three weeks.)

Spaying

If you are sure you do not wish your female to have puppies, you may consider spaying her. Contrary to common opinion, spaying does not have an unfavorable effect. In fact, early spaying can make a nervous female much more calm, gentle, affectionate. The spayed female will not become fat if you give her the proper diet and exercise.

The earlier spaying is done, the easier the operation will be. The ideal time for spaying is when the dog is fully developed, about six or seven months old. Do not delay your decision to spay your female until she is two or three years old; although the operation can be performed at any age, it can be harder on an older dog.

The Male Dog

The male dog has no season. He reaches his sexual maturity sometime between his eighth and twelfth month.

Do not feel that your male dog must be bred occasionally if he is to be happy. Unless he is a purebred dog whose pups will have some value, you are better off not breeding him.

Once a male dog has been bred he often becomes more nervous. Anxious to find a female, he may start roaming. For the unbred male dog you will always be the center of his world, all the happiness he requires.

Castration

Castration is usually not performed on a male dog unless there is a personality problem or unless his roaming resists other treatment. Castration can calm the temperamental, snappish male. The earlier it is performed the better, the ideal time being at about ten months.

Breeding Your Dog

If you would enjoy having a litter of puppies join your family and are prepared for all the work involved, the day will come when you decide to breed your female.

This decision should stem only from your desire to have her puppies. Do not be misled by any sentimental feeling that she will not be fulfilled until she has suckled a litter. She will be just as happy as she is. When you breed her you are letting her in for a lot of pain and hard work — don't feel you're doing her a big favor.

Mating with a stud

If your dog is a purebred, you will want to mate her with a purebred of the same breed. Most often this is done by finding a stud. The American Kennel Club, 51 Madison Avenue, New York, New York 10010, can supply you with information about breeders in your area. You may also be able to find a stud in the kennels listed in the yellow pages of your telephone book or in one of the many dog magazines. Stud fees range somewhere between fifty and two-hundred dollars, depending on the quality of the bloodlines. The owner of the stud takes care of mating arrangements.

Informal mating

If you wish to breed your dog with the dog of a friend, usually no money is asked. The owner of the male has the right to ask for "pick of the litter."

Before the dogs meet, you should be sure that both are in good health; your female should be examined for worms and checked for external parasites. Someone should stay with the pair during the mating to make sure that neither dog is injured, and that the breeding has been completed.

Mismating

If by chance your bitch has been mismated, a series of hormone injections after the mating will usually halt the pregnancy.

Care of the Pregnant Female

Once your female has been mated, keep her from all other males until her season is over, or she may present you with a mixed litter from several sires.

The mother dog will deliver puppies sixty to sixty-six days after she has become pregnant. She should be examined for worms before her third week (if she was not wormed before being mated). After three weeks of pregnancy, worming may cause her to abort.

As her appetite increases, give her more food, divided perhaps into several feedings. She should have a vitamin-mineral supplement, as prescribed by your veterinarian, and may also have milk if it agrees with her.

If her breasts become inflamed (about fifth week), soothe them with baby oil. You can feel the puppies about the sixth or seventh week. Do not poke or you may injure them. Run your fingers *gently* over the abdomen.

If she becomes constipated, which is often the case, avoid violent laxatives. They may cause a miscarriage. Instead, give her small doses of milk of magnesia. Do not let your dog get too fat, or her delivery may be difficult.

Your dog will be anxious and uncomfortable during pregnancy. She needs your gentle affection, but do not coddle her. She still should have her daily routine, including exercise. With the increased pressure on her abdomen, she will also need to be taken out more often to avoid accidents. Caution children to handle the mother-to-be gently.

The whole birth cycle is excellent education for children. A child will absorb the facts of life naturally through observing his or her pet in the various stages of pregnancy, and by asking questions.

Preparations for Delivery

At about the eighth week of pregnancy, start readying your dog for whelping. Alert your veterinarian in case you should need his help. Listen carefully to his expert instructions. (If you have a Pug, Pekinese, Boxer, or any variety with a blunt, square head, or any of the toy breeds, it might be better to take your dog to the veterinarian's for delivery. These breeds often have restricted pelvises, and consequently, difficult births.)

Prepare a whelping bed — a draft-free wooden box, large enough to allow her to move around easily (about one and one-half to two times her length). Make three walls high enough to protect the dogs from drafts, but one side low enough so the mother can get in and out. Cushion the floor with newspapers, making sure to change them frequently. Have the dog sleep in the box so she will be accustomed to it by the time her whelping date arrives.

The Whelping Day Arrives

You will know your dog is ready to whelp when you see her anxious pacing (later becoming frantic). She will whimper, pant, and strain. Guide her firmly but gently to the whelping box; she may try to make her nest elsewhere.

When the puppies start arriving, you will notice that each is born in a fetal sac. Hanging from the pup's navel will be the umbilical cord. Attached to that is the placenta through which he received nourishment. *Every pup that emerges must be followed by a placenta.* Be sure of this, or your dog will be in severe trouble.

The mother will remove each sac and consume it, licking the pup vigorously to start him breathing. Do not interfere unless you see the mother is not doing her job.

Assisting the mother

If all goes well, the mother needs no help during whelping. In rare cases, you may have to come to her aid.

When you see that your dog is in labor too long (actual hard labor of three or four hours) call your veterinarian: both mother and puppies can be injured by a long, painful labor.

When your dog is having difficulty giving birth to a pup, you can help her by covering your hand with a clean washcloth or small towel and gently lifting (not pulling) the pup's head from the mother. Don't jerk. She may have to be helped with a breech birth, when the pup's paws are presented first.

Removing the sac

Sometimes the mother does not remove the sac from the pups. Then you must do the job or the pup will suffocate. Work over a table; you are liable to drop the pup. Sterilize a pair of blunt scissors and cut the umbilical cord about one and one-half inches from the pup's navel. *Do not tie it.* Then place the puppy near the mother to be cleaned.

If the mother is unable to clean the pups, rub them vigorously with a terry towel. If a pup fails to breathe, this rubbing may get him started. If he still does not respond, shake the pup a little or swing him gently, head down, and wipe the inside of his mouth with a clean, dry washcloth.

Because the mother has only ten nipples, you may have to remove some of the pups of a larger-than-ten litter into a warm litter basket, where they can wait their turn for milk. Feed the smallest pups first — they are the weakest.

Now That the Pups Are Here

When the mother has finished whelping, she will rest. Feel gently around her abdomen to be sure all pups have been born. If you feel a lump or have any doubts, call your veterinarian promptly.

Give your dog a chance to go outside to relieve herself, then give her a snack of soft, easily digested food. A bowl of warm milk is usually a good starter.

On the second day you may give the mother her regular diet. She will need to eat often while nursing, probably three times a day, with an added snack at bedtime. She should also have supplementary minerals and vitamins while she is nursing.

Hand-feeding the puppies

If the mother doesn't have enough milk for her puppies, you may have to help out with extra bottle-feedings. The easiest formula is one cup milk, one teaspoon Karo, one egg yolk. For economy you may substitute equal parts of Carnation Evaporated Milk and water for the fresh milk.

Small puppies will have to be fed with doll babybottles and nipples, or eyedroppers; larger breeds can be fed with regular baby bottles.

Weaning
During the first few weeks the mother normally does most of the work — feeding, washing, cleaning up. About the third week you will notice the mother is getting tired of nursing. She will start vomiting up some of her partly digested food and have her pups eat it. This is a signal that it is time to start them on soft foods.

Weaning usually starts when the pups are three to five weeks old. You may start them on Friskies Puppy Food and milk or Puppy Food and formula, mixed to gruel consistency. The puppy may be fed soft foods

108 The Dog You Care For

twice a day at first, increasing the number of feedings to four or five after it is completely weaned — between four and six weeks. (See page 92, Feeding Your Puppy.)

As the pups are weaned, cut down on the mother's food supply to reduce her milk. Once pups are weaned, do not let them return to the breast. Keep the mother away from the pups until her milk has completely dried up.

Note: Swollen breasts are common during the drying-up period and seldom require treatment. If, however, you find the mother's breasts swollen and inflamed during nursing, you may suspect an infection. This can be painful to the mother and may lead to the death of any pup suckling it. Call your veterinarian for prompt treatment.

7

How To Travel With Your Dog

(And Not Wish You Had Stayed Home)

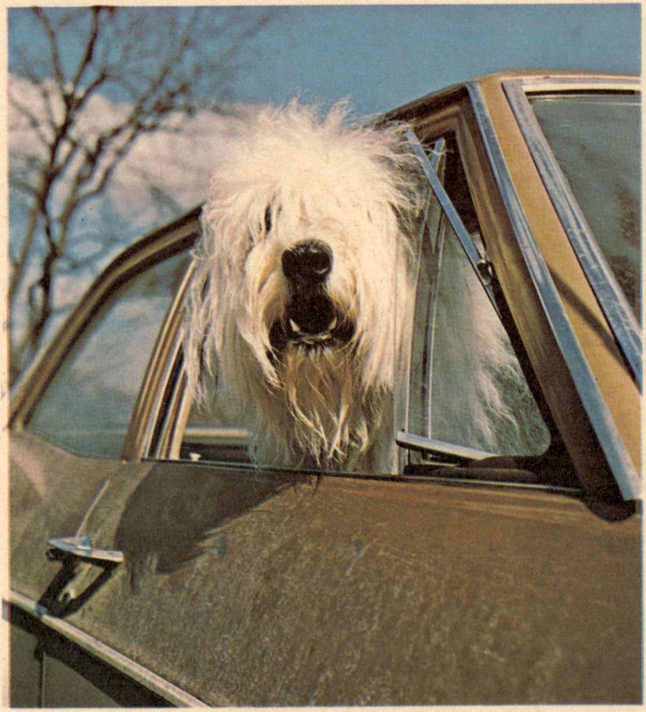

FOR many dog owners the thought of leaving doggy locked in a kennel is enough to spoil the trip. For others the thought of *bringing* doggy is enough to make them cancel altogether.

There is no reason these days why your dog — if you have trained him properly — cannot travel along with you and be part of the fun. But if you want a successful trip — one that your dog will enjoy too — some advance thought and preparation are necessary.

Traveling by Car

The grown dog usually loves automobile rides; he's often first in the car and raring to go. Car sickness is uncommon among dogs who have been accustomed to riding as pups.

Preparing your pup to be a traveler

If your dog is a pup, start with short drives to get him used to the motion. Do not feed him or give him water before the trips. After a few times out, he'll forget his nervousness and think the ride is fun.

The carrying case

While your dog is still a pup, and if he is a small breed, it might be well for you to accustom him to a dog carrier.

Put his blanket or toys in the carrier; then put him in a few times, leaving him there, but don't put on the lid or move the case. Later on, move the case a short distance with the lid off. Finally, when he can be moved happily in the carrier, put the lid on for short walks. When your pup is used to the carrier, be sure to put him in it once in a while so he won't forget about it. You *may* be able to take your pup in a carrier on a bus, train, or plane (but be sure to check with the line of your choice, as not all permit it) as well as in the car.

Car sickness

Some dogs, even though they enjoy traveling, are chronic whoopsers. It is wise to prepare for carsickness on a long trip by giving your dog a sedative such as sodium bromide (three to five grains), Dramamine, or Bonamine, as prescribed by your veterinarian.

Trunk travel

If your dog is not large, or if you have a station wagon, you may wish to take him in a crate where he can snooze in comfort. If you have no room for his crate in the car, you may have to put him in the trunk. This can be a comfortable spot for him provided you heed a few words of warning:

- Do not put your dog's crate in an open trunk compartment. It is far too cold and drafty. Also, your dog could be poisoned by carbon monoxide from the automobile's exhaust.
- Never put your dog in the trunk compartment with the lid closed, unless you make a large opening in the deck between the back of the rear seat and the rear window. (If your dog is not crated, you will want to cover this opening with wire mesh.)
- If you are carrying a dog in the trunk compartment, you must extend the exhaust pipe with a hose running upward.
- Remember that trunk travel is only for cool weather. In hot weather the car trunk, no matter how well ventilated, is too hot for your dog's safety.

Packing your dog's suitcase

Take along your pet's food and water pans and a supply of his regular food. A change of diet may upset him, especially when his routine has been disturbed by traveling. Also, take along jugs of drinking water; dogs are affected by water change. Pack his leash for exercising and a stout chain for securing him. You will also want to take a few old bath towels or some paper towels for wiping up in case of accidents.

Be sure your dog's license and identification tags are firmly attached to his collar before he starts out on a trip.

Hot weather travel

Dogs have much less tolerance for heat than humans do. Don't take chances with your dog's comfort. If the car is very hot, place your dog on a wet towel, putting another wet towel over him. Give him frequent drinks of cool water.

Parking your dog safely

If you leave your dog in the car when you eat or sight-see, be sure your car will be in the shade the *entire time* you are gone. Leave the windows rolled up, but open a few inches for ventilation. The side wings should also be left open. Leave a pan of water for your dog if you will be gone for some time. Never leash your dog when you leave him in the car — he could strangle himself.

Before you leave your dog, you'll be kind as well as wise to let him visit his own roadside restroom.

Make your dog a welcome guest

Not all hotels and motels accept dogs. Your best bet is to telephone or write ahead for reservations, booking them where you know your dog will be welcomed.

The hotel or motel management that will take in your pet deserves your courtesy. Don't let your pet run loose to soil the lawns or paths. Be sure your room is left without a trace of your dog's visit.

If you must leave the dog alone in the room, secure him with a stout chain or put him in his crate. Otherwise he may try to escape when the maid enters. Never leave windows open from the bottom — your pet may decide to do a little sight-seeing on his own.

If your dog damages anything in your room, be frank about it with the manager. Your consideration will help keep the "Dogs Allowed" sign polished — not only for you and your pet but for all those who follow.

Health certificates for travel in the United States

With the exception of New York, all states require a certificate of health issued by a licensed veterinarian of the state of origin, stating that the dog is in good health, free of all infectious and communicable diseases, and comes from an area free of rabies. The majority of states also require a certificate stating that the dog has been vaccinated against rabies within six months.

Although these requirements are for the dog who will be living in the state for a month or more, it is advisable to take health and rabies certificates along, even if your stay may be only a few days in each state. In the first place, should you have to put your dog in a kennel overnight, you will undoubtedly need such certificates. And second, if your dog should bite someone or be bitten by another animal, you will have saved yourself much worry and trouble by having proof of inoculation.

Traveling by Air

Because airlines, railroads, and steamships may vary in their policies regarding transportation of dogs, it is better to check with several carriers before making arrangements for travel.

Every major airline will transport your dog. Check with the carrier of your choice to determine its requirements and facilities for shipping your animal safely and comfortably. A health certificate is required before the dog is shipped out of the state. If you plan to use a small airline, call the cargo traffic manager to see if the line ships dogs.

Well in advance of your trip you should write or call the cargo traffic manager of the airline you intend to use, or check with your travel agent to find out the following:

- What papers your dog must have and to whom they should be presented.
- If you can take your dog into the cabin of the airplane, and if so, what preparations must be made.
- If insurance is available for your dog.
- If the dog must be shipped as freight or excess baggage, and if so

1. What are the charges?
2. What type of carrier must he be in?
3. Will the dog be on the same plane with you?
4. Will you need to reserve space?
5. When and where will he be delivered?

6. Is it a direct flight, or are there stopovers?
7. What arrangements are available for food, water, blankets, first aid?
8. Will the dog be properly cared for during possible stopovers?

Traveling by Ship

Almost every major shipping line will make provision for transporting your dog. Before you make your own travel reservations, call the general passenger department (or the freight department if you are shipping him alone) with these questions:

- What ships on this line transport dogs?
- What papers (medical and legal) must the dog have?
- To whom should these papers be given if you are traveling with the dog? If the dog is traveling without you?
- Can the dog go into your cabin?
- Does the ship have a veterinarian?
- When should passage for the dog be booked? When should the dog arrive at the dock?
- How much does it cost to ship him?
- Should he be insured?

Traveling by Train

All major railroads will transport dogs. When you begin to make arrangements you may find it helpful to ask the following questions of the baggage agent (or have your travel agent do so):

- What are the charges for taking a dog?
- Are you allowed to take him with you on a coach or in a compartment? If you are allowed to keep the dog with you, are there short "doggy" stops for exercise? (Many trains provide these.)
- Must the dog be in a carrier?
- What provisions are necessary if the dog is to be shipped as baggage?

If you are going to ship your dog, be sure he travels in a comfortable crate — like one of these.

- Do you need a baggage car reservation? To whom is the dog delivered? Where is he picked up?
- Is insurance necessary?
- What facilities does the railroad have for feeding, watering, and keeping the dog warm or cool?

Traveling Abroad

Laws and regulations governing entrance of dogs must be checked for each country you plan to visit. Long before your departure date you should call your veterinarian to see if he has an up-to-date list of requirements for each country. Then, write to the nearest consulate of each country on your itinerary. The consulate will provide you with an import permit, any recent changes in the regulations, and procedural instructions (such as number of copies of papers to be furnished, who will validate the health certificate, etc.).

Quarantines

Hawaii, England, Ireland, Scotland, and the Scandinavian countries, as well as several others, require that your dog be kept in quarantine after arrival. Periods of time vary with each country. If you are planning to stay a year or more it may be worth the trouble of quarantine to have your dog come with you.

For further information on traveling abroad with your pet, write to the Department of Agriculture, Washington, D. C.

SUMMING IT ALL UP

There's a lot to remember in what has been discussed, and a lot to put into practice. Keep this book handy — read it over a number of times so that you can recall information you may need when the occasion arises. We suggest you keep the book with your dog's medicines where it will be handy in case of emergency.

Because you want your dog to be well cared for, well behaved, but most of all, happy, we suggest that you keep the following points in mind:

- Be sure your home is safe inside and out.
- Never let a dog near busy streets without a leash.
- Be conscientious about training your dog properly — never allow his behavior to become a problem.
- Keep shots up-to-date. Remember, the veterinarian is your dog's best friend.
- Never let your female roam free in season. Allow a dog to mate only when you know the puppies will have good homes.
- Never neglect your dog's grooming — it is important to his health.
- Find a totally balanced diet of quality prepared commercial dog food and stick with it.
- Never travel with a dog unless you can prepare properly for his comfort and safety.

You will be repaid many times over for the care and love you give your dog — repaid in fun, companionship, loyalty, and devotion.

A few of the trophies awarded to Friskies champion dogs, Carnation Research Kennels, Carnation Farms, Washington (photo courtesy of Carnation Company)

VITAL STATISTICS AND HEALTH RECORD

*Paste in Picture
of Your Dog Here*

Dog's Name

OWNED BY

*Name*_____

*Address*_____

*City*_____ *State*_____ *Zip*_____

BACKGROUND DATA

Date of Birth _____

122   The Dog You Care For

Date Acquired _____

Breed _____

Sex _____

Color and Markings _____

Registration No. _____

Sire _____

Dam _____

Breeder _____

HEALTH RECORD AND DATA

WORMS

First Worming - Date _____

Other Wormings - Date _____

Types of Worms _____
                    (Identified by Veterinarian)

Medicine _____
                    (Prescribed by Veterinarian)

SHOTS

Temporary Shots - Date _____

            For _____

VACCINATIONS

Hepatitis - Date _____

Vital Statistics And Health Record

Distemper - Date _____

Rabies - Date _____

Leptospirosis - Date _____

UNSPAYED FEMALES

Dates in Season _____

FEEDING DATA

Weaned - Age of Dog _____

Number of Feedings Daily _____

Type of Foods _____

_____

_____

REMINDER NOTES _____

_____

_____

_____

_____

_____

_____

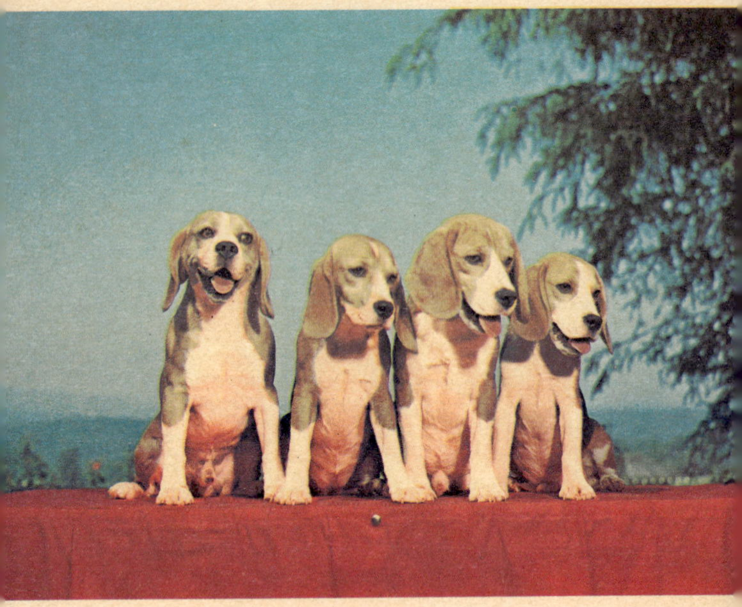

INDEX

Abrasions, treatment of, 68
Accidents, 66-75
    first-aid kit, 65
Age, compared to man, 64
Air travel, 115-116
American Kennel Club, 101
    registration, 29
Anemia, 58
Antidote for poison, 73
Artificial respiration, 67
Automobile accident, 68
Barking, 37
Bathing, 81-82
    see also Grooming
Bed, 19-20
Bee sting, treatment of, 68
Behavior, see Training
Behavior problems, 37-39
Bitch, 99
    see also Female
Biting, 48
Breeding, 99-108
Bruises, treatment of, 69
Brushing, 79-81
Burns, treatment of 69
Car
    accident, 68
    chasing, 47-48
    sickness, 112
    travel, 111-112
Care of new dog, 15-20
Carnation Research Laboratories, 88-89
Carrying case, 111
Castration, 100

Cat or dog bite, treatment of, 69
Champion Bardene Bingo, 88
Chemical burns, treatment of, 69
Children and dogs, 15, 18
Choosing a dog, 15-16
Clipping
    in summer, 80
    sick dog, 60
Coat, 58-59, 79-80, 86
Collar, 22, 40
Coma, from poisoning, 73
Combing, see Grooming
"Come," teaching to, 45
Commands, see Training
Constipation, 62, 65, 70, 103
Convulsions, symptoms and treatment, 70
Curb-training, 35-36
Cuts, treatment of, 70
DDT in flea powder, 58-59
Destructiveness, 49-50
Diarrhea, 59, 62, 71
Dietary deficiency, 48
Digging, 53
Discipline, 18
    see also Training
Distemper shots, 57
Dog food, see Feeding, Food
Dog house, 20-22
Dog or cat bite, treatment of, 69
Dog repellents, 53
Dogfights, 50

125

Index

"Doggy" odor, 82
"Down," teaching, 46
Droppings, eating, 48
Drowning, 71
Ears, care of, 81, 82
Electric shock, 25
    treatment for, 71
Equipment for dog, 22
Emergency treatment, 66-67, 68-75
Exercise, 35, 53, 113
External parasites, 58-59
Eyes, care of, 81, 82
    injury to, 71
Feeding, 85-96
    amount, 91
    balanced diet, 87-88
    modified diets, 60, 90
    old dog, 96
    puppy, 90, 92-93
    self-feeding, 90
    water, 90
    weaning, 92, 107
Feeding dish, 22
Female, 15, 99-106
Fetal sac, 105-106
Fighting, 50
First aid, 68-75
    first-aid kit, 65
Flea powder, 58-59
Fleas, 58-59
Food
    as reward, 35, 40
    kinds, 85-87, 88-89
    see also Feeding
Food fallacies, 85-87
Foreign objects in throat, 25, 72
Foreign travel, 117
Formula, 92
Fractures, treatment of, 72

Friskies Nutrition Research Kennels, 88-89
Frostbite, treatment of, 72
Grooming, 79-82
Hand-feeding puppies, 106
Health, 17, 23, 57-75
    see also Feeding, Grooming
Health certificate, 121
"Heat," 19, 113
Heatstroke or sunstroke, 20
    symptoms and treatment, 75
"Heel," teaching to, 42
Hepatitis shot, 57
Hotels, 114
House-training, 34
Humane society, 47
Illness, 60-65
    care during, 62-63
    symptoms of, 62
Indigestion, treatment of, 72
Injury, care and first aid, 66-67, 68-75
Inoculations, see Shots
Internal parasites, 59-60
Jumping up, breaking habit, 53
Labor, signs of, 105
Leash, leashing-training, 22, 39, 41
Leaving dog alone, 37, 52
Leptospirosis shot, 57
Lice, 58
License, 27-28
Liquid medicine, administering, 64
Loneliness, 19, 51-52
Lost dog, 26-27
Male, 100, 101
Mange, 58
Mating, 100-102
Maturity, sexual, 100

Medicine, administering, 63-64
    dosage, 65
Mismating, 102
Mites, 58
Motels, 114
Muzzle, mouth tie, 63
Nails, care of, 80-81
Name, 34
New dog, care of, 17-27
Nose temperature, 62
Nursing, 106
Nutrition, 88-89
Obedience, see Training
Obedience schools, 47
Objects in throat, treatment for, 72
Odor
    "doggy," 82
    skunk, 74
Old dog, 38, 64-65, 96
Over-affectionate dog, the, 52-53
Overwatchfulness, 20
Paper-training, 34-35
Parasites, 58-60
Pills, administering, 63-64
Placenta, 105
Poison ivy, treatment of, 73
Poisoning, 25, 65, 73
Porcupine quills, treatment for, 73
Pregnancy, 103-104
Puppy, 15, 17, 18
    feeding, 92, 94-95
    leash-training, 39
    newborn, 105-106
    shots, 57
    weaning, 93, 107-108
Quarantines, travel, 118
"Quiet," teaching to be, 37-39
Rabies shots, 57

Registration, AKC, 29
Rewards, 35, 40
Roaming, 51
Safety, 23-26
Scratching, see Skin disorders
Season, 15, 99
Selection of dog, 15-16
Self-feeding, 90
Shelter, outdoor, 20-22
Shock, electric, treatment for, 71
Shock, symptoms and treatment of, 74
Shots, 57
"Sit," teaching to, 43, 44
Skin disorders, 60
    see also Grooming
Skunk odor, treatment for, 74
Sleeping, 19-20
Snake bite, treatment for, 74
SPCA, 47
Spaying, 99-100
Sprain, treatment of, 75
"Stand," teaching to, 45-46
"Stay," teaching to, 44-45
Stud, 101
Suffocation, treatment for, 75
Sunstroke or heatstroke, 26, 75
Tapeworm, 58
Teeth, care of, 81, 86
Temperature, how to take, 62
Ticks, 58
Toenails, care of, 80-81
Toys, 22-23
Train travel, 116-117
Training, 33-53
    breaking bad habits, 37-39
    house-training, 34-35
    leash, 39, 40

Index

obedience, 41, 42-43, 44-46
rewards, 35, 40
Travel, 111-118
"Turn," teaching to, 42-43
Umbilical cord, 106
Unconsciousness, treatment for, 75
Vaccination, 57
Veterinarian, 23, 58, 61, 62
Wandering, 51
Watchdog, 37, 39
Water, 90
Weaning, 93, 107-108
Whelping, 104-105
Worming bred female, 103
Worms, 58-60, 85-86
Wounds, treatment of, see First-aid chart, 68-75